Study Guide
To Accompany

Abnormal Psychology
Tenth Edition

Ann M. Kring
University of California - Berkeley

Gerald C. Davidson
University of Southern California

John M. Neale
State University of New York at Stony Brook

Sheri L. Johnson
University of Miami

Prepared by:
Douglas Hindman
Eastern Kentucky University

WILEY
JOHN WILEY & SONS, INC.

Cover Photo: ©Ted Kinsman/Photo Researchers

To order books or for customer service please, call 1-800-CALL WILEY (225-5945).

ISBN-13   978- 0-471-74297-5
ISBN-10   0-471-74297-X

Printed in the United States of America

10 9 8 7 6 5 4 3 2 1

Printed and bound by Courier Kendallville

To My Students

This Study Guide is designed to help you study *Abnormal Psychology, 10th Edition* by Davison & Kring. Each chapter in this guide provides a variety of aids to make your studying easier and more effective.

Overview sections place the chapter in context by describing its relationship to the chapters that precede and follow it.

Chapter Summary sections, not surprisingly, summarize the chapter.

Learning Goals identify the important ideas or concepts to be learned in the chapter.

Key Terms provide a place for you to write in definitions of technical words introduced in the chapter. Typically, these terms are boldfaced in the text.

Study Questions are questions for you to answer as you read each section of the text. The Study Guide provides space for you to write your answers to each question. Research indicates that actually filling in the answers is an effective way to study.

Self-Test provides a way for you to check your knowledge of the chapter. The Self-Test questions cover the content specified by the Study Questions, except for an occasional asterisked (*) test question.

Internet Resources provides websites to begin additional study on the topics in the chapter. Additional general websites are at the end of the Introduction.

The Study Guide begins with a chapter on *Studying in This Course (and in Other Courses Too)*. This chapter is based on my experiences helping my students improve their study skills. It describes a study method (SQ4R) you can use to improve your study skills. It also provides suggestions for coping with common study problems. I hope you'll find this chapter helpful.

Abnormal psychology is a fascinating, but complex, topic for many students. Hopefully, this Study Guide will make your studying easier and more effective. It is based on the experiences, comments, and criticisms of hundreds of students who have used it in my classes. I invite you to join them in offering suggestions for further improvements.

Douglas Hindman
Berea, Kentucky

CONTENTS

Introduction   Studying in This Course (and in Other Courses Too)
                        SQ4R System   vii
                        Study Problems   ix
                        Internet Resources   xiii

Chapter 1   Introduction and Historical Overview
                        Overview   1
                        Study Questions   7
                        Self-Test   11

Chapter 2   Current Paradigms in Psychopathology
                        Overview   15
                        Study Questions   21
                        Self-Test   25

Chapter 3   Diagnosis and Assessment
                        Overview   29
                        Study Questions   33
                        Self-Test   38

Chapter 4   Research Methods in the Study of Psychopathology
                        Overview   43
                        Study Questions   47
                        Self-Test   51

Chapter 5   Anxiety Disorders
                        Overview   55
                        Study Questions   60
                        Self-Test   65

Chapter 6   Somatoform Disorders and Dissociative Disorders
                        Overview   69
                        Study Questions   72
                        Self-Test   76

Chapter 7   Stress and Health
                        Overview   81
                        Study Questions   84
                        Self-Test   88

Chapter 8   Mood Disorders
                        Overview   93
                        Study Questions   99
                        Self-Test   105

Chapter 9   Eating Disorders
             Overview   109
             Study Questions   111
             Self-Test   115

Chapter 10   Substance-Related Disorders
             Overview   119
             Study Questions   124
             Self-Test   129

Chapter 11   Schizophrenia
             Overview   133
             Study Questions   137
             Self-Test   141

Chapter 12   Personality Disorders
             Overview   145
             Study Questions   148
             Self-Test   152

Chapter 13   Sexual and Gender Identity Disorders
             Overview   157
             Study Questions   161
             Self-Test   165

Chapter 14   Disorders of Childhood
             Overview   169
             Study Questions   171
             Self-Test   178

Chapter 15   Late Life and Psychological Disorders
             Overview   183
             Study Questions   186
             Self-Test   190

Chapter 16   Psychological Treatment
             Overview   195
             Study Questions   198
             Self-Test   202

Chapter 17   Legal and Ethical Issues
             Overview   207
             Study Questions   210
             Self-Test   214

Introduction:
Studying in This Course
(and in Other Courses Too)

Overview

I'm convinced, though it might be hard to prove, that few students get bad grades because they're dumb. There is little in the average college curriculum (including abnormal psychology) that's beyond the intellectual capacities of most college students. I'm convinced most students get poor grades because they don't know how to study.

Being a student is a job. The hours are long and the pay is terrible, but it's still a job. The payoff is the knowledge you gain and the grades you get. You've been at this "job" for many years, and you're probably not through with it. If this is to be your job, you might consider how to become really good at it. Are you learning? Are you working efficiently and getting the results you should?

This Study Guide incorporates features to help you develop good study skills. If you spend a little time consciously working on your study skills, you can help the process along.

This chapter is intended to help you review and improve your study skills. The first part of the chapter describes a system, SQ4R, which you can use in this, or almost any, course. The second part of the chapter contains suggestions for dealing with common study problems.

The SQ4R Study System

The following is one variation of a study method called "SQ4R" (Survey, Question, Read, Write, Recite, Review). If you're not used to it, it may seem a bit complicated at first. If you check around, though, you will find that the "good" students are already using it or a similar system. Research shows that SQ4R works. It takes a bit of extra effort to get used to, but remember that studying is a skill and that learning any skill (like typing, driving, and playing ball) takes time and practice. You will find, though, that your efforts will pay off in both this and your other courses.

As you begin to study a new chapter, use the following steps:

Survey

First, survey the entire chapter briefly. Spend a few minutes getting a general idea of the material. Look over the titles, pictures, introduction, and summary in the text. Read the overview, chapter summary, and essential concepts in this Study Guide. While doing so, ask yourself what you will be studying. Figure out how the text is organized to cover the topic. Don't read the chapter in detail yet. This brief survey will help you focus your attention and become familiar with new vocabulary and concepts. Research suggests that initially surveying the chapter can reduce your overall study time by 40%.

Question

Take the first portion of the chapter and ask yourself what you are about to study. The study questions in this Study Guide will help you formulate this question. In other courses, take the main heading or topic and turn it into a question.

Read

Then, read the first portion of the text looking for the answer to your question. It is important that you actively seek the answer as you read. Deliberately try *not* to read every word. Instead, read for answers.

Typically a text will make several points regarding each general topic. Look for words indicating these points such as, "first," "furthermore," or "finally". Generally a paragraph contains one idea. Additional paragraphs may elaborate on or illustrate the point. You may find it helpful to number each point in the text as you find it.

Write

Write down the answer in the space below the study question in your guide. In other courses, take study notes. This step is critical. By writing the answer you confirm that you actually understand it. Occasionally, when you try to write down your answer, you'll discover you don't understand the idea well enough to put it into words. That's okay. Go back and read some more until you figure it out.

As you write the answer, strive to use as few words as possible. Being concise is important. Try to come up with a few key words that convey the idea. When you can condense a long portion of text into a few key words that express the whole idea, you know you understand the concept clearly. The few key words you write down will be meaningful to you so you will remember them. Do not write complete sentences or elaborate excessively. The fewer words you can use, the better you probably understand and will remember the concept.

When you finish, go on to the next study question. Read, write, and repeat until you finish.

Recite

After you finish the chapter, go back and quiz yourself. Do this aloud. Actively speaking and listening to yourself will help you remember. Look at each question and try to repeat the answer without looking. Cover your answers with a sheet of paper so you don't peek accidentally. If you've done the earlier steps well, this won't take much time.

Review

Set aside a few minutes every week to recite the material again. Put several questions together and try to recite all the answers to a whole general topic. Do this regularly and you'll find it takes little time to refresh yourself for an exam.

Get with a classmate and quiz each other, or ask a friend to read the questions and tell you if your answers make sense. This step helps you understand (not just memorize) the ideas. As you discuss answers with someone else, you develop new ways of looking at the material. This can be especially helpful when the test questions aren't phrased quite the way you expected.

Coping with Study Problems

The previous section of this chapter described an active study technique that has proven useful to many students. This section talks about common study problems and what to do about them.

Finding the Time

Does it seem like you never have time to study — or that you study all the time and still aren't getting results? Admittedly, study takes time, but let's look at the matter.

The traditional rule of thumb is that you should study two hours outside class for every hour in class. If that sounds like a lot, consider this: the average college student's class load is 15 semester hours. If you study two hours for each class hour, that's 30 additional hours for a "work week" of 45 hours.

If you have trouble finding that 45 hours, it's time to look at how you spend your time. Make a "time log". You can copy the time log at the end of this chapter or make one of your own. Use it to record how you spend your time for a week or so. Don't try to change what you're doing. Just record it.

After a week or so, review your log to see how you're using your time. There are 90 hours between 8 A.M. and 11 P.M. in a six-day week. If you devote half those hours to the "job" of being a student, you'll have 45 hours left. It's your time.

You may want to schedule your time differently. You'll need to decide what works for your style and situation. If you set up a schedule, be sure to include time for things you really enjoy as well as time to eat, do your laundry, etc.

Schedule adequate study time and actually spend it studying. If you get everything done and have time left over, use it to get ahead in one of your classes. When your study time is over, you should be able to enjoy other activities without worrying about your "job".

Getting Started

Do you find it difficult to actually get down to work when it's study time? Many students find it helpful to find or make a specific "study place". It could be a desk in your room, the library, or any place where you won't be disturbed and will have access to your books and materials.

Use your study place *only* to study. If it *has* to be a place where you do other things, change it in some way when you use it to study. For example, if you use the kitchen table, clear it off and place a study light on it before you start to study. If you're interrupted, leave your study place until the interruption is over and you can return to studying.

If you do this, you'll soon get into the habit of doing nothing but studying in your study place and will be able to get to work as soon as you sit down.

Reading the Material

Some students believe that effective study means to "read the chapter" three or four times. This could be called the "osmosis approach" to studying. You expose yourself to the words in the text and hope something will soak in — like getting a suntan. This approach does *not* work.

If you just "read the chapter," you'll often realize you've been looking at words but have no idea what they mean. If you come to a difficult idea, you're likely to skip over it. When you reread the chapter, you're likely to recall that the idea was difficult and skip over it again. The result is that you end up having read the chapter three or four times without understanding most of it.

Instead, use an active study technique like the SQ4R system described earlier. Research indicates that active study techniques can dramatically increase how quickly you learn material and how much of it you recall.

Underlining the Text

Many students underline (or highlight) their texts. Underlining works well — sometimes. For most people, underlining is not as efficient as taking notes. The danger in underlining is that you tend to underline things to be learned later rather than learning them now. Thus, you can end up with half the chapter underlined and none of it learned. If you *must* underline, try to underline as few words as possible in the same way as the "key words" approach described in the "Write" section earlier. Avoid used textbooks that someone else underlined. The previous owner may have been a poor underliner. More importantly, the value of underlining (like the value of taking notes) is in doing it yourself and in learning what's important in the process.

Reading Speed

Slow reading can lead to a number of problems. Most obviously, it takes too long to get through the material. More importantly, you lose interest before you get to the main point. You forget the first part of an idea before you get to the end. (You "lose the forest for the trees".) You may not understand a concept unless it's clearly stated in one sentence. You may misinterpret material because you take so long getting through it that you start reading in your own ideas.

If this description sounds familiar, you might want to check your reading speed. To check your speed, time yourself while you read for exactly five minutes. Estimate the total words you've read and divide by five. To estimate the total words you read, count the number of words in five lines and divide by five to get the average number of words per line. Then count the number of lines you read and multiply by the number of words per line.

For textbook material, an efficient reading speed is about 350 to 400 words per minute — depending on the difficulty of the topic and your familiarity with it. For novels and other leisure reading, many students can read 600 to 800 words per minute and "speed readers" can read much faster. Remember that understanding and flexibility in your reading style is more important than mere speed. But, often, increased speed actually improves your understanding.

You can increase your reading speed to some extent by conscious effort. If you watch someone read, you'll notice that their eyes move in "jerks" across the line. Our eyes can read words only when stopped. We read a group of words, move our eyes, read the next group, and so on. To increase reading speed, try to take in more words with each eye stop. Don't be concerned with every "and" or "but". Try to notice only words that carry meaning. Read for ideas, not words. If you read very slowly, you should consider seeking special help. Most campuses have reading laboratories where you can get help in increasing your reading speed. Ask your instructor or advisor if your school offers such help.

Analyzing Tests

Perhaps you studied hard, but still did poorly on the test. How can you make sure the same thing doesn't happen again?

You'll find it helpful to analyze what went wrong on each question you missed. You may be able to do this in class, or you may need to see your instructor individually.

Compare the test and your study notes or Study Guide answers. Examine each question you got wrong and reconstruct what happened. For example, did you have the answer in your notes? If so, why didn't you recognize it on the test? Do this for each question you got wrong and look for a pattern. Here are some possibilities.

Was the answer not in your study notes at all? Perhaps you didn't answer all of a study question or, otherwise, missed important concepts. Perhaps you should talk to your instructor about his or her orientation to the course. What concepts or areas does he or she consider important? What does the instructor want you to learn? Ask the instructor to review your notes and point out where you omitted things he or she considers important.

If your study notes seem complete, go back and compare them to the text. Perhaps you misread the text, got the concept wrong, or only got part of it. Make sure you read the entire section of the text. Sometimes the first sentence of a paragraph only *seems* to convey the idea. Later sentences (or paragraphs) may really convey the core theme. Perhaps, also, you need to read faster. Slow readers often have trouble with complex concepts that aren't clearly stated in one sentence.

Perhaps the answer was in your study notes but you didn't remember it on the test. You can be pleased that you had it in your notes — but why didn't you remember it? Were you too tense? Do you need to recite and review more?

Perhaps you knew the answer but didn't recognize it because of the way the question was phrased. That suggests you're stressing memorization too much. Try to review with someone else. Have your partner make you explain your answers and discuss ways they would say it differently. This will help you understand ideas when they are stated differently.

More Help

Many schools have a learning lab or learning skills center where you can get individualized help. Ask your instructor what facilities your school provides.

For ideas on using this time log, see "Finding the Time," page ix.

Time Log

Date _____

Time	Doing what?	Where?	Comments
7:00 -	-	-	
7:30 -	-	-	
8:00 -	-	-	
8:30 -	-	-	
9:00 -	-	-	
9:30 -	-	-	
10:00 -	-	-	
10:30 -	-	-	
11:00 -	-	-	
11:30 -	-	-	
12:00 -	-	-	
12:30 -	-	-	
1:00 -	-	-	
1:30 -	-	-	
2:00 -	-	-	
2:30 -	-	-	
3:00 -	-	-	
3:30 -	-	-	
4:00 -	-	-	
4:30 -	-	-	
5:00 -	-	-	
5:30 -	-	-	
6:00 -	-	-	
6:30 -	-	-	
7:00 -	-	-	
7:30 -	-	-	
8:00 -	-	-	
8:30 -	-	-	
9:00 -	-	-	
9:30 -	-	-	
10:00 -	-	-	
10:30 -	-	-	
11:00 -	-	-	
11:30 -	-	-	
12:00 -	-	-	

Internet Resources

The following are general Internet resources on abnormal psychology and related topics. Additional Internet resources at the end of each chapter cover topics of that chapter.

Information Sources

Allpsych Online offers information on a wide range of psychological topics.   www.allpsych.com

American Assoc. of Family Physicians offers information on a wide range of psychological as well as medical health topics.   http://www.aafp.org

At Health offers online information for mental health professionals and consumers.www.athealth.com

Gradschools.Com has information on graduate programs in psychology and other fields.
www.gradschools.com

Healthfinder has wide ranging health information from the US Department of Health and Human Services.   healthfinder.gov

Mental Help Net has links and information for mental health consumers.   www.mentalhelp.net

Mental Health InfoSource has information and links on most psychological disorders and an "Ask an Expert" service.   mhsource.com

National Institute of Mental Health is a government agency with information and resources on mental health for professionals and consumers.   www.nimh.nih.gov

National Mental Health Association provides consumer-oriented information on mental health and disorders, recent mental health news, and links to their local community groups.   www.nmha.org

National Mental Health Information Center is a US Government center for mental health and substance abuse information.   www.mentalhealth.org

Neurosciences on the Internet has links to a wide range of information on neuroscience topics.
neuroguide.com

Neuropsychology Central has links to information on human neuropsychology.
neuropsychologycentral.com

New York Access to Health is organized by New York City libraries and has a wide range of information on health and disorders.   www.noah-health.org

Psych Central provides mental health information, support, and links to online resources.
psychcentral.com

Psych Watch has links to a wide range of websites for psychologists and psychology students.
www.psychwatch.com

Psychology Information Online has a wide range of information on psychological problems and treatment including finding a provider and starting therapy.   www.psychologyinfo.com

Research Help

PubMed is the public medical research database of the National Library of Medicine. It covers much of the social science literature and has links to full text articles.

www.ncbi.nlm.nih.gov/entrez/query.fcgi

American Psychological Association Databases permits searching their extensive research databases for a fee. One option is 24 hours of searching for $11.95.   www.apa.org/science/lib.html

Social Psychology Network is a database of thousands of articles and online resources in social psychology.   www.socialpsychology.org

American Academy of Family Physicians allows web searches of its journals for mental health related topics.   www.aafp.org

Professional Organizations

American Counseling Association   www.counseling.org

American Psychological Association   www.apa.org

American Psychological Society   www.psychologicalscience.org

American Psychoanalytic Association.   www.apsa.org

Association for the Advancement of Behavior Therapy.   www.aabt.org

American Mental Health Counselors Association   www.amhca.org

International Coach Federation (personal coaches)   www.coachfederation.org

Just for Fun

Journal of Polymorphous Perversity is an irreverent psychology humor magazine.
www.psychhumor.com

1 Introduction and Historical Overview

Overview

The first four chapters cover basic ideas and issues in abnormal psychology. These chapters are the background for the rest of the text, which covers the various forms of psychopathology and related topics.

The first two chapters discuss viewpoints on the nature of psychopathology. Chapter 1 introduces psychopathology and how views on it have developed over time. Chapter 2 continues with current paradigms or views regarding psychopathology

The way we view problems becomes especially important when discussing ways of classifying and studying psychopathology, which are covered in Chapters 3 and 4. Chapter 3 introduces the standard classification system, *The Diagnostic and Statistical Manual of Mental Disorders* as well as methods and issues in assessment. Chapter 4 describes research methods in abnormal psychology.

The theoretical viewpoints and research approaches discussed in these first four chapters form a foundation for studying specific forms of psychopathology starting in Chapter 5. The bulk of the book reviews the major forms of psychopathology. The last two chapters deal with treatment and legal/ethical issues in more detail.

Chapter Summary

What is Abnormal Behavior The study of psychopathology is a search for the reasons why people behave, think, and feel in abnormal—unexpected, sometimes odd, and possibly self-defeating—ways. Unfortunately, people who exhibit abnormal behavior or have a mental illness are often stigmatized. Reducing the stigma associated with mental illness remains a great challenge for the field.

In evaluating whether a behavior is abnormal, psychologists consider several different characteristics, including personal distress, disability, violation of social norms, and dysfunction. Each characteristic tells something about what can be considered abnormal, but none by itself provides a fully satisfactory definition. The DSM-IV-TR definition includes all of these characteristics.

History of Psychopathology Since the beginning of scientific inquiry into abnormal behavior, supernatural, biological, and psychological points of view have vied for attention. More supernatural viewpoints included early demonology, which posited that mentally ill people are possessed by demons or evil spirits, leading to treatments such as exorcism. Early biological viewpoints originated in the writings of Hippocrates. After the fall of Greco-Roman civilization, the biological perspective became less prominent in Western Europe, and demonological thinking gained ascendancy, as evidenced by the persecution of so-called witches. Beginning in the fifteenth century, mentally ill people were often confined in asylums, such as Bethlehem; treatment in asylums was generally poor or nonexistent, until various humanitarian reforms were instituted. Early systems of classifying mental disorders led to a reemergence of the biological perspective in the eighteenth and nineteenth centuries. In the twentieth century, genetics and mental illness became an important area of inquiry, though the findings from genetic studies were used to the detriment of the mentally ill during the eugenics movement.

Contemporary Thought Psychological viewpoints emerged in the nineteenth century from the work of Charcot and the seminal writings of Brewer and Freud. Freud's theory emphasized stages of psychosexual development and the importance of unconscious processes, such as repression and defense mechanisms that are traceable to early-childhood conflicts. Therapeutic interventions based on psychoanalytic theory make use of techniques such as free association and the analysis of transference in attempting to overcome repressions so that patients can confront and understand their conflicts and find healthier ways of dealing with them. Later theorists, such as Jung and Adler, made various modifications in Freud's basic ideas and emphasized different factors in their perspectives on therapy.

Behaviorism suggested that behavior develops through classical conditioning, operant conditioning, or modeling. B. F. Skinner introduced the ideas of positive and negative reinforcement and showed that operant conditioning can shape behavior. Behavior therapists try to apply these ideas to change undesired behavior, thoughts, and feelings.

Mental Health Professions There are a number of different mental health professions, including clinical psychologist, counseling psychologist, psychiatrist, psychoanalyst, social worker, and psychopathologist. Each involves different training programs of different lengths and with different emphasis on research, psychological assessment, psychotherapy, and psychopharmacology.

Learning Goals

1.   Be able to explain the meaning of stigma as it applies to people with mental illness.

2.   Be able to describe and compare different definitions of abnormality.

3.   Be able to explain how the causes and treatments of mental illness have changed over the course of history.

4.   Be able to describe the historical forces that have helped to shape our current view of mental illness, including biological, psychoanalytic, and behavioral views.

5.   Be able to describe the different mental health professions, including the training involved and the expertise developed.

To My Students

Before you plunge into this study guide, take a few minutes to understand it. After all, a study guide is a tool, and tools are most useful if you learn to use them properly.

This study guide comes out of my experience of what helps my students in abnormal psychology. It is designed to help them, and you, learn the material more effectively and efficiently.

The introductory chapter in this guide (entitled *Studying in This Course*) describes how to study effectively and provides suggestions for common study problems. Studying is a skill that can be learned. Read the introductory chapter for ideas on how to improve your own study skills.

For each chapter of the text, begin by reading the *Overview, Chapter Summary,* and *Learning Goals* sections in this guide. These sections provide a broad outline of the chapter and how it fits into the overall text. That information will improve your studying later by helping you see how various details are part of broader topics.

The *Key Terms* section lists new technical terms introduced in the chapter. There is space for you to write in definitions, which is an excellent way for you to learn and study these terms.

The *Study Questions* provide a guide for studying the chapter by identifying the important ideas in each part. Read the first question, then study the indicated pages looking for the answer. Write notes on the answers you find in the space provided. Review these notes later for tests.

The *Self-Test* provides multiple-choice and short-answer questions you can use to test your knowledge.

Internet Resources provides some websites for you to begin searching out additional information on topics in the chapter. Additional resources are at the end of the introduction chapter.

I hope you will enjoy and benefit from your study of abnormal psychology and this study guide. I welcome your comments, criticisms, and suggestions. Please feel free to write me at the address on the title page.

Key Terms

Psychopathology (p. 3)

Stigma (p. 3)

Abnormal behavior (p. 4)

Harmful dysfunction (p. 6)

Demonology (p. 8)

Exorcism (p. 8)

Asylums (p. 10)

Moral treatment (p. 12)

General paresis (p. 15)

Behavior genetics (p. 15)

Electroconvulsive therapy [ECT] (p. 16)

Cathartic method (p. 17)

Psychoanalytic theory (p. 18)

Psyche (p. 18)

Id (p. 18)

Libido (p. 18)

Unconscious (p. 18)

Pleasure principle (p. 18)

Ego (p. 18)

Reality principle (p. 18)

Superego (p. 18)

Oral Stage (p. 18)

Anal stage (p. 19)

Phallic stage (p. 19)

Latency period (p. 19)

Genital stage (p. 19)

Fixation (p. 19)

Oedipus complex (p. 19)

Electra complex (p. 19)

Defense mechanism (p. 20)

Repression (p. 20)

Psychoanalysis (p. 20)

Free association (p. 20)

Transference (p. 20)

Interpretation (p. 21)

Analytical psychology (p. 21)

Collective unconscious (p. 21)

Individual psychology (p. 22)

Behaviorism (p. 23)

Classical conditioning (p. 23)

Unconditioned stimulus (UCS) (p. 23)

Unconditioned response (UCR) (p. 23)

Conditioned stimulus (CS) (p. 24)

Conditioned response (CR) (p. 24)

Extinction (p. 24)

Law of effect (p. 24)

Operant conditioning (p. 24)

Positive reinforcement (p. 25)

Negative reinforcement (p. 25)

Shaping (p. 25)

Modeling (p. 26)

Behavior therapy (p. 26)

Counterconditioning (p. 26)

Systematic desensitization (p. 26)

Aversive conditioning (p. 26)

Clinical psychologists (p. 27)

Psychotherapy (p. 28)

Counseling psychologists (p. 28)

Psychiatrists (p. 28)

Psychoactive medications (p. 28)

Psychoanalyst (p. 28)

Social workers (p. 28)

Psychopathologist (p. 28)

Study Questions

What is Abnormal Behavior? (p. 4-6)

1.   Briefly describe four characteristics of abnormality. Explain the strengths and weaknesses of each in defining abnormality. How does the text suggest viewing these characteristics and abnormality generally? (p. 4-6)

History of Psychopathology (p. 7-13)

2.   Describe demonology and early biological approaches to the causes of deviant behavior. How did each explain abnormality? What kinds of treatment resulted from these explanations? (p. 7-8)

3.   According to many historians, how did views and treatment of mental illness change during the Dark Ages and change again starting in the thirteenth century? What evidence suggests that the mentally ill were considered witches — and what evidence suggests they were not? (p. 8-10)

4.   Describe the development of asylums for the mentally ill during the fifteenth and sixteenth centuries. How were the mentally ill treated in these early asylums?   How did this change under Pinel's reforms? (p. 10-11)

5.   Describe the development of moral treatment under Tuke and others. How did this approach view and treat mental illness? Why was this approach largely abandoned? (p. 11-13)

The Beginning of Contemporary Thought (p. 14-27)

6.   Describe an early classification system. Describe the beginning of contemporary biological views of mental problems by describing three areas of biologically based work. (p. 14-16)

7.   Describe the beginning of contemporary psychological views by describing the work of Mesmer, Chariot, and Brewer. How did their work lead Freud to psychoanalysis? (p. 16-17)

8.   Summarize Freud's view of the structure of the mind (three functions or energies), his four (or five) stages of psychosexual development, and the role of defense mechanisms. (p. 17-20)

9. What does psychoanalysis attempt to do overall? Describe three basic psychoanalytic techniques? Describe the key concepts of two neo-Freudians and of humanistic and existential psychology. (p. 20-23)

10. What is the basic approach of behaviorism? Describe three types of learning and the basic concepts of each. Explain how each could lead to forms of psychopathology. Describe three early behavior therapy techniques with an example of each. (p. 23-27)

The Mental Health Professions (p. 27-28)

11. Describe the training and skills of six mental health professions. For clinical psychologists, include the distinctions between Ph.D. and Psy.D. training. (p. 27-28)

Self-Test, Chapter 1

(* Items not covered in Study Questions.)

Multiple Choice

*1.   The study of psychopathology deals most directly with
       a. the development of asylums.
       b. the theories and treatments developed by followers of Freud.
       c. the nature and development of mental disorders.
       d. theories derived from animal laboratories.

2.   Ted, who has a fear of snakes, quit his job when he was asked to relocate to the Southwest
      (where snakes are more common). This is an example of which definition of abnormal
      behavior?
       a. anxiety
       b. disability
       c. statistical infrequency
       d. violation of norms

3.   The first theory of deviant behavior attributed the behavior to
       a. demonic possessions.
       b. dysfunctional learning experiences.
       c. excessive black bile.
       d. hypochondria.

4.   Which of the following was not one of the four humors Hippocrates believed maintained
      psychological health?
       a. black bile
       b. red bile
       c. yellow bile
       d. blood

5.   John was receiving treatment for mental illness. He lived during the Dark Ages. Who was most
      likely treating him?
       a. a psychiatrist
       b. a monk
       c. an asylum worker
       d. he was not receiving treatment during the Dark Ages.

6.   Early medical treatment of the mentally ill in asylums in Europe
       a. could be characterized as inhumane.
       b. was a radical revision of the American approach as it involved more personal choice on the
          part of the patient.
       c. symbolized the beginning of humane treatment and scientific inquiry into mental illness.
       d. utilized the Freudian method.

7.   The early classification system developed by Kraepelin
       a. proposed two major groups of severe mental illnesses.
       b. was not influential in later diagnostic manuals.
       c. argued that not all disorders had a biological basis.
       d. assumed all disorders had the same genesis.

8.   Carl Jung proposed that all people have a repository of information that allows for an understanding of our ancestors. This is called the
     a. personal unconscious.
     b. collective unconscious.
     c. unified unconscious.
     d. symbolic unconscious.

9.   Jimmy, age 5, runs to the door every time he hears a car drive by, expecting his mother to come home from work. From a classical conditioning perspective, the sound of the car is
     a. an unconditioned response.
     b. an unconditioned stimulus.
     c. a conditioned response.
     d. a conditioned stimulus.

10. According to the law of effect
     a. Tommy will stop misbehaving at home if he is sent to his room.
     b. Kim will continue reading if reinforced after each time she is interested in reading.
     c. Tony will readily learn new task by observing someone else.
     d. only a and b are correct.

Short Answer

1.   What is a limitation of defining abnormality as a violation of social norms?

2.   What evidence suggests that the "witches" of the thirteenth century were actually mentally ill?

3.   What did Philippe Pinel do and why was it important in the history of psychopathology?

4.   Why was moral treatment largely abandoned?

5.   Why was general paresis and syphilis important in the history of biological approaches to psychopathology?

6.   How was Breuer's work important to the development of Freudian psychoanalysis?

7.   In Freudian psychoanalysis, what is the role or function of the ego?

8. Describe the behavior therapy technique of systematic desensitization.

9. Describe the difference between the Ph.D and the Psy.D. in the training of applied psychologists.

10. What is the difference between a psychologist and a psychiatrist in terms of their training and professional practice activities?

Internet resources

The following are Internet resources to begin exploring the topics in this chapter. Additional general Internet resources are at the end of the introduction chapter.

Today in the history of Psychology offers a database of significant events in the history of psychology on any date. Amaze your professor!   www.cwu.edu/~warren/today.html

Careers in Psychology and lots of other information for psychology students is available from the American Psychological Association.   www.apa.org/students

Library research in Psychology offers a wide range of literature databases and reference information on psychological topics.   www.apa.org/science /lib.html

Gradschools.Com has information on graduate programs in psychology and other fields.   www.gradschools.com

Answers to Self-Test, Chapter 1

Multiple Choice

1. c (p. 3)   2. b (p. 5)   3. a (p. 7-8)   4. b (p. 8)
5. b (p. 8-9)   6. a (p. 10-11)   7. a (p. 14-15)   8. b (p. 21-22)
9. d (p. 23-24)   10. d (p. 24)

Short Answer

1. People with some problems (like anxiety) do not appear to be different (i.e. do not violate norms). Others (like criminals) violate norms but are not considered "crazy". Also, norms vary across cultures. (p. 5)

2. Their "confessions" included delusions and hallucinations such as flying to secret cult meetings. (Of course other evidence suggests the witches were not mentally ill.) (p. 9)

3. Pinel (or his assistant) was first to remove the chains from asylum patients and treat them humanely. He was important because he showed decent care could lead to recovery. (p. 11-12)

4. Public hospitals became too large to provide individual care. Physicians gained control and shifted focus to biological factors. (p. 12-13)

5. Important because general paresis was widely considered a form of mental illness with many theories of its psychological cause. Then it was shown to have a biological cause (syphilis) giving credibility to the biological approach. (p. 15)

6. Breuer's cathartic method showed that people could "forget" traumatic past events and that remembering them was helpful. This suggested that unconscious memories were important in treatment. (p. 17-18)

7. The ego deals with reality in order to satisfy the urges of the id. That is, the ego figures out how to cope with the world in such a way that the id's desires are, ultimately, fulfilled. (p. 18)

8. Clients are taught to deeply relax. Then, while relaxed, they are exposed to gradually more feared situations. Thus they learn to stay relaxed in previously feared situations. (p. 26)

9. Ph.D. training emphasizes scientific study of human behavior and applying that knowledge to practice. Psy.D. training emphasizes study of applied skills of assessment and intervention with less research emphasis. (p. 27-28)

10. Psychologists are trained in psychology while psychiatrists are trained in medicine. Psychologists typically apply psychological knowledge in assessment, psychological testing, psychotherapy, etc. Psychiatrists typically apply medicine in prescribing psychoactive medications. (p. 28)

2 Current Paradigms in Psychopathology

Overview

This is the second of four introductory chapters covering topics that are basic to the rest of the text. Chapter 1 discussed the role of paradigms in science generally and traced the paradigms that have been important in the history of psychopathology. Many of the differences underlying those paradigms are still unresolved. In particular, the relationship between physical and psychological factors in pathology is still widely debated. As the field has developed, other distinctions have also emerged. Such distinctions underlie the current paradigms that are described in Chapter 2. These current paradigms will be used to help understand and study the various types of psychopathology described later in the text.

Chapters 3 and 4 will deal with the topics of assessing and studying psychopathology. They describe the current categories of psychopathology, methods of assessing it, and research methods in studying it. There are a number of issues and controversies involved in both assessing and studying pathology. Not surprisingly many of these reflect differences among the various paradigms presented in Chapters 1 and 2.

After Chapter 4, the text will begin eleven chapters covering the major forms of psychopathology.

Chapter Summary

Scientific inquiry is limited by scientists' human limitations and by the limited state of our knowledge: people see only what they are able to see, and other phenomena go undetected because scientists can discover things only if they already have some general idea about them.

A paradigm is a conceptual framework or general perspective. Because the paradigm within which scientists and clinicians work helps to shape what they investigate and find, understanding paradigms helps us to appreciate subjective influences that may affect their work.

Several major paradigms are current in the study of psychopathology and therapy. The choice of a paradigm has important consequences for the way in which abnormal behavior is defined, investigated, and treated.

Genetic Paradigm The genetic paradigm holds that psychopathology is caused or at least influenced by heritable factors. Recent genetic findings show how genes and the environment interact, and it is this type of interaction that will figure most prominently in psychopathology.

Neuroscience Paradigm The neuroscience paradigm emphasizes the role of the brain, neurotransmitters, and other systems, such as the HPA axis. Biological treatments attempt to rectify the specific problems in the brain or to alleviate symptoms of disorders, often using drugs to do so.

The psychoanalytic paradigm derives from the work of Sigmund Freud. The more contemporary contributions of this paradigm are primarily in treatment, including ego analysis and brief therapy. Although Freud has been criticized, the psychoanalytic paradigm continues to influence the field by highlighting the importance of childhood experiences, the unconscious, and the fact that the causes of behavior are not always obvious.

Cognitive Behavioral Paradigm The cognitive behavioral paradigm emphasizes schemas, attention, and irrational interpretations and their influence on behavior as major factors in psychopathology. In both practice and theory, the cognitive behavioral paradigm has usually blended cognitive findings with the behavioral in an approach to intervention that is referred to as cognitive behavioral. Cognitive behavior therapists such as Beck and Ellis focus on altering patients' negative schemas and interpretations.

Factors that Cut Across Paradigms Emotion plays a prominent role in a number of disorders. It is important to distinguish among components of emotion that may be disrupted, including expression, experience, and physiology. Emotion disturbances are the focus of study across the paradigms.

Sociocultural factors, including culture, ethnicity, gender, social support and relationships are also important in conceptions of psychopathology: the prevalence and meaning of disorders may vary by culture and ethnicity; men and women may have different risk factors for different disorders; and social relationships can be an important buffer against stress. Sociocultural factors are now being considered in the work of geneticists, neuroscientists, psychoanalysts, and cognitive behaviorists.

Diathesis-Stress Because each paradigm seems to have something to offer to our understanding of mental disorders, it is important to develop more integrative paradigms. The diathesis–stress paradigm, which integrates several points of view, assumes that people are predisposed to react adversely to environmental stressors. The diathesis may be genetic, neurobiological or psychological and may be caused by early-childhood experiences, genetically influenced personality traits, or sociocultural influences among other things.

To My Students

I urge you to pay particular attention to this chapter.

The paradigms in Chapter 2 will be used in discussing the various forms of abnormality presented throughout the text. By getting a clear understanding of each paradigm now, you'll find it much easier to make sense of the more detailed discussions later.

In addition, these are present-day paradigms. Try to identify which of them best fits your own personal paradigm (assumptions) about abnormality. This will help you recognize and evaluate your own inclinations throughout the course.

Learning Goals

1.   Be able to describe the essentials of the genetic, neuroscience, psychoanalytic, cognitive-behavioral, and diathesis-stress paradigms.

2.   Be able to describe the concept of emotion and how it may be relevant to psychopathology.

3.   Be able to explain how culture, ethnicity, and social factors figure into the study and treatment of psychopathology.

4.   Be able to recognize the limits of adopting any one paradigm and the importance of integration across multiple levels of analysis.

Key Terms

Paradigm (p. 29)

Genetic paradigm (p. 30)

Gene expression (p. 30)

Polygenic (p. 31)

Heritabiliity (p. 31)

Shared [and nonshared] environment (p. 31)

Genes (p. 31)

Behavior genetics (p. 31)

Genotype (p. 31)

Phenotype (p. 31)

Diathesis (p. 32)

Molecular genetics (p. 32)

Allele (p. 32)

Polymorphism (p. 32)

Linkage analysis (p. 33)

Genetic marker (p. 33)

Gene-environment interaction (p. 33)

Serotonin transporter gene (p. 34)

Reciprocal gene-environment interaction (p. 35)

Neuroscience paradigm (p. 36)

Neuron (p. 36)

Nerve impulse (p. 37)

Synapse (p. 37)

Neurotransmitters (p. 37)

Reuptake (p. 37)

Dopamine (p. 37)

Norepinephrine (p. 37)

Serotonin (p. 37)

Gamma-aminobutyric acid [GABA] (p. 37)

Second messengers (p. 38)

Agonist (p. 38)

Antagonist (p. 38)

Corpus callosum (p. 38)

Grey matter (p. 38)

Frontal lobe (p. 38)

Parietal lobe (p. 38)

Temporal lobe (p. 38)

Occipital lobe (p. 38)

White matter (p. 39)

Ventricles (p. 39)

Thalamus (p. 39)

Brain stem (p. 39)

Cerebellum (p. 39)

Anterior cingulate (p. 40)

Septal area (p. 40)

Hippocampus (p. 40)

Hypothalamus (p. 40)

Amygdala (p. 40)

Pruning (p. 40)

Somatic nervous system (p. 40)

Autonomic nervous system [ANS] (p. 40)

Sympathetic nervous system (p. 40)

Parasympathetic nervous system (p. 40)

HPA axis (p. 42)

Cortisol (p. 42)

Psychoanalytic paradigm (p. 44)

Psychotherapy (p. 45)

Ego analysis (p. 45)

Brief therapy (p. 46)

Cognitive behavioral paradigm (p. 47)

Time-out (p. 47)

Token economy (p. 47)

Exposure (p. 47)

In vivo (p. 47)

Cognition (p. 48)

Schema (p. 48)

Cognitive behavior therapy [CBT] (p. 50)

Cognitive restructuring (p. 50)

Rational-emotive behavior therapy [REBT] (p. 50)

Emotions (p. 52)

Diathesis-stress (p. 55)

Study Questions

The Genetic Paradigm (p. 30-35)

1.   Describe the former and the contemporary views on the relation of genetic and environmental influences on behavior. Describe the following basic concepts in the genetic paradigm: gene expression, heritability, and shared/nonshared environment. (p. 30-31)

2.   Distinguish between two approaches in the genetic paradigm. For the first, explain the relationship between genotype, phenotype, and diathesis. For the second, describe three research approaches. Explain (with examples) and distinguish between two kinds of gene-environmental interactions. Evaluate the genetic paradigm in two points (genes/environment and challenge). (p. 31-35)

The Neuroscience Paradigm (p. 36-43)

3.   Describe the role of neurons and neurotransmitters in transmitting nerve impulses. Describe two views on the link between neurotransmitters and psychopathology. (p. 36-38)

4.   Identify the major structures of the brain and their functions. (p. 38-40)

5.   Describe the role of the autonomic nervous system and the neuroendocrine system including their important components.   What is the usual neuroscience approach to treatment and what are two reasons to be cautious about it?   Evaluate the neuroscience paradigm by defining reductionism and the problem with reductionism including examples. (p. 40-43)

The Psychoanalytic Paradigm (p. 44-47)

6.   What is the central assumption of the psychoanalytic paradigm?   Give two reasons that little research has been done to support this paradigm.   Describe ego analysis and how it differs from traditional psychoanalysis. Evaluate the Psychoanalytic paradigm by listing three criticisms and three continuing impacts. (p. 44-47)

The Cognitive Behavioral Paradigm (p. 47-51)

7.   Identify two roots of the cognitive behavioral paradigm. For the first, briefly describe four therapy techniques from this approach and one criticism. For the second, briefly describe three contributions noting how the second and third are related. (p. 47-50)

8.   What is the general approach of cognitive behavior therapy?   Illustrate this approach by describing the contemporary views of Beck and Ellis. Evaluate this approach by explaining how cognitive concepts and therapy approaches are often unclear. (p. 50-51)

Factors that Cut Across the Paradigms (p. 52-55)

9.   Identify two sets of factors that cut across the paradigms.   Explain the importance of emotions. Describe three components of emotion with examples. Define epidemiological studies as an approach to studying socio-cultural factors. Briefly discuss the sociocultural factors of quality of relationships, cultural factors, and ethnic factors. (p. 52-55)

Diathesis-Stress: An Integrative Paradigm (p. 55-57)

10.   Describe the diathesis-stress paradigm as a way to integrate other paradigms. Give examples of how diatheses could involve neurological factors, psychological factors, or the interactions among them. What kind of events might be stressors?   List three key points of this paradigm. (p. 55-57)

Self-Test, Chapter 2

(* Items not covered in Study Questions.)

Multiple Choice

1.   Which of the following statements is true?
     a. Scientists have recently concluded that nature is more important than nurture.
     b. Scientists have recently concluded that nurture is more important than nature.
     c. For most psychological disorders, nature guides 70% of behavior, while nurture guides the remaining 30%.
     d. Almost all behavior is heritable to some degree, but the environment shapes what genes are expressed.

2.   Whereas the _____ changes over time, the _____ is fixed at birth.
     a. genotype; phenotype
     b. phenotype; genotype
     c. zygote; dizygote
     d. monozygotic type; dizygotic type

3.   Which of the following statements is false?
     a. Psychological disorders involve many genes.
     b. Linkage analysis is an important method of molecular genetics.
     c. Psychological disorders most likely involve a small subset of genes.
     d. "Knockout studies" are useful for understanding the role of specific genes.

4.   The way in which genes promote certain types of environments is called
     a. gene-environmental interaction.
     b. reciprocal gene-environment interaction.
     c. epigenetics.
     d. environmental interaction.

5.   A nerve impulse is
     a. the gap between sending and receiving brain cells.
     b. a change in electric potential within the cell.
     c. the genotypic features of the cell.
     d. chemical substances called neurotransmitters.

* 6.   A drug that is a serotonin agonist
     a. stimulates serotonin receptors.
     b. blocks serotonin receptors.
     c. releases second messengers.
     d. is most likely a drug for treating schizophrenia.

* 7.   Which of the following is often referred to as the "stress hormone"?
     a. serotonin
     b. GABA
     c. testosterone
     d. cortisol

8. Behaviorism and behavior therapy have often been criticized for minimizing which of the following factors?
    a. thinking and feeling
    b. dreams
    c. unconscious desires
    d. early childhood experiences

9. Contemporary emotion theorists suggest that emotions are comprised of a number of components including
    a. moods, affect and experiential components.
    b. thoughts, actions and affective components.
    c. fear, sadness and mood.
    d. expressive, experiential and physiological components.

10. According to the diathesis-stress model
    a. ultimately, the diathesis is the driving force in the development of disorders.
    b. ultimately, environmental stressors are the driving force in the development of disorders.
    c. both diathesis and stress are necessary in the development of disorders.
    d. some people are more likely to be influenced by a diathesis, while others are more likely to be influenced by stress.

Short Answer

1. Define heritability and how it is commonly misunderstood.

2. Describe two views on the link between neurotransmitters and psychopathology.

3. Where is the thalamus and what is its function?

4. Define reductionism.

5. Give two reasons there has been little formal research on psychoanalysis.

6. Identify three continuing impacts of Freud and psychoanalysis.

7. Describe the behavior therapy technique of "token economy".

8.   How would a therapist using Ellis's cognitive therapy approach deal with Helen, a college
      student who is extremely anxious about her grades?

9.   How are cognitive behavioral concepts often unclear?

10.   Describe the diathesis-stress paradigm.

Internet Resources

The following are Internet resources to begin exploring the topics in this chapter. Additional general
Internet resources are at the end of the introduction chapter.

American Psychoanalytic Association has lots of information on contemporary psychoanalytic
issues and views, as well as links to many other psychoanalytic websites.   www.apsa.org

Association for Advancement of Behavior Therapy is the major national organization for cognitive
and behavioral therapists.   The website has information on careers, therapy approaches, and
therapists.   www.aabt.org

Answers to Self-Test, Chapter 2

Multiple Choice

1. d (p. 30)	2. b (p. 31)	3. c (p. 33)	4. b (p. 35)
5. b (p. 37)	6. a (p. 38)	7. d (p. 42)	8. a (p. 48)
9. d (p. 52)	10. c (p. 56)		

Short Answer

1. Heritability is the extent to which a behavior or disorder within a population can be attributed to genetic factors. It is commonly misunderstood as applying to individuals. It is not the percent of an individual's disorder which is due to heredity. (p. 31)

2. One view looks at the amount of neurotransmitter perhaps because of problems in processing it. The other looks at sensitivity to the neurotransmitter: for example, receptor sites that are too numerous or too easily excited. (p. 37)

3. The thalamus is located in the middle of the brain and is the relay center for all the senses except olfaction. (p. 39)

4. Reductionism is the idea that things can or should be reduced to more basic elements. For example, that behavior should be understood in terms of brain activity. (p. 43)

5. Psychoanalysis is difficult to study because of its many vague concepts. Also, psychoanalysts have focused more on treatment. Indeed, the theory grew out of observations during treatment. (p. 46)

6. Importance of (a) childhood, (b) unconscious influences on behavior, (c) non-obvious factors in behavior. (p. 46-47)

7. In a token economy some concrete token (like a sticker) is given for correct behavior. The token can be exchanged for some reinforcer (candy, fun activity, etc.) (p. 47)

8. Ellis would suspect Helen is demanding high grades of herself; believing she "must" or "should" get grades rather than deciding if she "wants" grades and determining how to do so. (p. 50)

9. Cognitive behavioral concepts often are not clearly defined and do not clearly explain how problems develop. (p. 50)

10. Diathesis-stress looks for both predispositions (diatheses) and current life issues (stresses) to a disorder. Thus, it focuses on interactions among multiple factors to understand disorders. (p. 55)

3 Diagnosis and Assessment

Overview

This is the third of four introductory chapters. The first two chapters covered historical and contemporary paradigms or viewpoints on psychopathology. Chapters 3 and 4 deal with less overtly theoretical topics. Chapter 3 summarizes the standard diagnostic system for classifying disturbed behavior as well as methods and issues assessment. Chapter 4 will cover research methods and completes the introductory chapters. While Chapters 3 and 4 are less overtly theoretical, paradigm differences continue and are reflected in issues about how best to classify and study psychopathology.

Chapter 5 begins eleven chapters on the major forms of pathology. Finally the last two chapters will deal with psychological treatment and legal/ethical issues.

Chapter Summary

In gathering diagnosis and assessment information, clinicians and researchers must be concerned with both reliability and validity. Reliability refers to whether measurements are consistent and replicable; validity refers to whether assessments are tapping into what they are meant to measure. Assessment procedures vary greatly in their reliability and validity. Certain diagnostic categories are more reliable than others.

Diagnosis Diagnosis, the process of assessing whether a person meets criteria for a mental disorder, is a critical aspect of the field of abnormal psychology. Having an agreed-on diagnostic system allows clinicians to communicate effectively with each other and facilitates the search for causes and treatments. Clinically, diagnosis provides the foundation for treatment planning.

The Diagnostic and Statistical Manual of Mental Disorders (DSM), published by the American Psychiatric Association, is an official diagnostic system widely used by mental health professionals. A revision of the fourth edition of the manual, referred to as DSM-IV-TR, was published in 2000. An important feature of the current DSM is its multiaxial organization. In the multiaxial classification system of DSM, Axes I and II make up the mental disorders per se; Axis III lists any physical disorders believed to bear on the mental disorder in question; Axis IV is used to indicate the psychosocial and environmental problems that the person has been experiencing; and Axis V rates the person's current level of adaptive functioning.

Some critics of the DSM argue against diagnosis in general. They point out that diagnostic classifications may ignore important information and may also increase stigma. Specific shortcomings of the DSM have also been identified. These include the high rates of comorbidity, the reliance on a categorical classification system, limited reliability for some disorders, and questions about the validity of a few of the diagnostic categories. Most researchers and clinicians, though, recognize that the DSM is an enormous advance compared to historical systems.

Assessment Clinicians rely on several modes of psychological and neurobiological assessment in trying to find out how best to describe a client, search for the reasons the patient is troubled, arrive at an accurate diagnosis, and design effective preventive or remedial treatments. Regardless of what assessment method is used, it inevitably reflects the paradigm of the clinician. The best assessment involves multiple types of methods.

Psychological assessments include clinical interviews, assessments of stress, psychological tests, and behavioral and cognitive assessments.

Clinical interviews are structured or relatively unstructured conversations in which the clinician probes the patient for information about his or her problems. Assessing stress is key to the field of abnormal psychology. Despite difficulties with defining stress, a number of useful methods for assessing it have been developed, including the LEDS and ADE.

Psychological tests are standardized procedures designed to assess personality or measure performance. Personality assessments range from empirically derived self-report questionnaires, such as the Minnesota Multiphasic Personality Inventory, to projective tests in which the patient interprets ambiguous stimuli, such as the Rorschach Test. Intelligence tests, such as the Wechsler Adult Intelligence Scale, evaluate a person's intellectual ability and predict how well he or she will perform academically.

Behavioral and cognitive assessment is concerned with how people act, feel, and think in particular situations. Approaches include direct observation of behavior; interviews and self-report measures that are situational in their focus; and specialized, think-aloud cognitive assessment procedures that attempt to uncover beliefs, attitudes, and thinking patterns related to specific situations.

Neurobiological assessments include imaging techniques, such as fMRI, that enable us to see various structures and access functions of the living brain; neurochemical assays that allow clinicians to make inferences about levels of neurotransmitters; neuropsychological tests, such as the Halstead–Reitan, which seek to identify brain defects based on variations in responses to psychological tests; and psychophysiological measurements, such as heart rate and skin conductance, which are associated with certain psychological events or characteristics.

Cultural and ethnic factors play a role in clinical assessment. Assessment techniques developed on the basis of research with Caucasian populations may be inaccurate when used with clients of differing ethnic or cultural backgrounds, for example. Clinicians can have biases when evaluating ethnic minority patients, which can lead to minimizing or exaggerating a patient's psychopathology. Clinicians use various methods to guard against the negative effects of cultural biases in assessment.

Learning Goals

1.   Be able to describe the purposes of diagnosis and assessment.

2.   Be able to distinguish the different types of reliability and validity.

3.   Be able to identify the basic features, strengths, and weaknesses of the DSM-IV-TR.

4.   Be able to describe the goals, strengths, and weaknesses of psychological and neurobiological approaches to assessment.

5.   Be able to discuss the ways in which culture and ethnicity impact diagnosis and assessment.

Key Terms

Reliability (p. 62)

Interrater reliability (p. 62)

Test-retest reliability (p. 62)

Alternate-form reliability (p. 62)

Internal consistency reliability (p. 62)

Validity (p. 62)

Content validity (p. 62)

Criterion validity (p. 62)

Concurrent validity (p. 62)

Predictive validity (p. 63)

Construct validity (p. 63)

Diagnostic and Statistical Manual of Mental Disorders [DSM-IV-TR] (p. 64)

Multiaxial classification system (p. 65)

Comorbidity (p. 71)

Categorical classification (p. 71)

Dimensional diagnostic systems (p. 72)

Clinical interview (p. 75)

Structured interview (p. 76)

Stress (p. 78)

Psychological tests (p. 79)

Personality inventory (p. 79)

Standardization (p. 79)

Minnesota Multiphasic Personality Inventory [MMPI] (p. 79)

Projective test (p. 81)

Projective hypothesis (p. 81)

Thematic Apperception Test [TAT] (p. 82)

Rorschach Inkblots (p. 82)

Intelligence test (p. 84)

Behavioral observation (p. 86)

Behavioral assessment (p. 86)

Self-monitoring (p. 86)

Ecological momentary assessment [EMA] (p. 86)

Reactivity (p. 87)

CT or CAT scan (p. 90)

Magnetic resonance imaging [MRI] (p. 90)

Functional magnetic resonance imaging [fMRI] (p. 90)

BOLD (p. 90)

PET scan (p. 90)

Metabolite (p. 91)

Neurologist (p. 92)

Neuropsychologist (p. 92)

Neuropsychological tests (p. 93)

Psychophysiology (p. 94)

Electrocardiogram [EKG] (p. 94)

Electrodermal responding (p. 94)

Electroencephalogram [EEG] (p. 94)

Study Questions

Cornerstones of Diagnosis and Assessment (p. 61-63)

1. Define reliability and validity, (p. 62) explaining the relationship between them. Define four kinds of reliability and three kinds of validity. In particular, explain why construct validity is more complex. (p. 62-63)

Classification and Diagnosis (p. 63-73)

2.   What are the five axes in DSM-IV-TR and the rationale for distinguishing them (especially Axes I and II)? Describe four changes designed to improve the reliability and validity of recent versions of DSM. Describe three ways that ethnic and cultural considerations are incorporated into DSM-IV-TR. (p. 63-70)

3.   Summarize four criticisms of DSM, each with two or three sub-points. Identify two criticisms of diagnosis in general. (p. 71-73)

Psychological Assessment (p. 74-88)

4.   Identify four different approaches to assessment (on p. 75, 79, 84, and 85). In practice, how are these approaches used in assessing a person? Briefly describe four general characteristics of clinical interviews (answering questions, paradigm, rapport, and structure). What are structured interviews, such as the SCID, and what is their advantage? (p. 75-77)

5.   The text covers three techniques for the assessment of stress. Describe each technique and explain how it handles problems with earlier techniques. (p. 78-79)

6.   Regarding psychological tests, what is standardization? As a self-report personality inventory describe the MMPI including how it was developed and modified, and its use of validity scales. (p. 79-81)

7.   What is the assumption behind projective tests?   Describe two projective tests especially Exner's scoring system for the Rorschach.   What were IQ tests originally designed to measure and how else are they used? Describe their reliability and (two kinds of) validity. (p. 81-85)

8.   How do behavioral and cognitive assessments differ from more traditional methods? Describe four approaches with an example of each. (p. 85-88)

Neurobiological Assessment (p. 88-95)

9.   List and define four areas of neurobiological assessment.   Describe four methods of brain imaging and the advantages/disadvantages of each.   Describe four methods of neurotransmitter assessment and the problems with the last two. Identify three general problems with both brain imaging and neurotransmitter assessment approaches. (p. 89-92)

10.   Distinguish between the interests of neurologists (who might use brain imaging and neurotransmitter assessment) and neuropsychologists.   How do neuropsychological tests provide information about brain functioning?   Briefly describe two neuropsychological tests. Define psychophysiology and describe three psychophysiological measures.   As a final cautionary note identify four issues with all neurobiological methods. (p. 92-95)

Cultural and Ethnic Diversity and Assessment (p. 96-98)

11. How can cultural bias be a factor in assessment tests and in clinicians' evaluations?   Describe three strategies for avoiding cultural bias. Why should clinicians be particularly tentative when drawing conclusions about patients from other cultures? (p. 96-98)

Self-Test, Chapter 3

(* Items not covered in Study Questions.)

Multiple Choice

1. Sophie is taking a personality test. The test has items that are all closely related to one another. This is an example of
    a. external validity.
    b. internal consistency.
    c. internal validity.
    d. test-retest reliability.

2. In addition to having Panic Disorder, Tony has hypertension. The clinician diagnosing him thinks that his medical condition is affecting his psychiatric symptoms. Where, if at all, would his hypertension be included in the DSM-IV-TR diagnosis?
    a. axis II
    b. axis III
    c. axis IV
    d. The medical condition would not be included in the DSM-IV diagnosis.

3. One important way in which the DSM-IV-TR is an improvement from previous editions of the DSM is because
    a. DSM-IV-TR includes paranoid personality disorder.
    b. DSM-IV-TR allows for multiple diagnoses.
    c. DSM-IV-TR is more culturally sensitive.
    d. it is the first edition to exclude the diagnosis of homosexuality.

4. An alternative to the DSM has been suggested where diagnoses are based upon
    a. exclusively theory-driven criteria.
    b. ratings along dimensions.
    c. an accumulation of symptoms that describe different diagnostic entities.
    d. none of the above choices have been suggested as alternatives to the DSM.

5. What type of validity is considered the most important for diagnosis?
    a. content
    b. reliability
    c. construct
    d. inter-rater

* 6. According to the American Psychological Association, which of the following is <u>not</u> an appropriate way in which to describe a person with a mental illness?
    a. schizophrenic
    b. person with depression
    c. individual with a learning disorder
    d. person with bipolar disorder

* 7. Why is it important to measure levels of stress in psychological assessments?
    a. Stress is central to many disorders.
    b. Stress can contribute to heart disease.
    c. Stress can be defined more accurately than other symptoms.
    d. Stress is very objective.

* 8.   Support for the criterion validity of the MMPI-2 is based upon findings of
   a. concordance between the MMPI-2 and other objective personality tests.
   b. high correlations between the MMPI-2 and performance on projective personality tests.
   c. high agreement between the diagnoses rendered from the MMPI-2 and those obtained from other clinical sources.
   d. low correlations between the MMPI-2 and intelligence tests.

9.   Which of the following is <u>least</u> likely to be used in behavioral assessment?
   a. projective tests
   b. clinical interviews
   c. self-report inventories
   d. physiological measures

10.   Cultural diversity should lead clinicians to
   a. avoid using most tests with individuals from other cultures.
   b. adhere strictly to DSM criteria in making diagnoses.
   c. only treat individuals with whom they share the same cultural background.
   d. seek information on various cultural practices and views.

Short Answer

1.   Dr. Jones has just developed the new diagnostic label of "Sprangfordism". How will he demonstrate the construct validity of this label?

2.   Give several examples of dimensional systems for classifying people.

3.   Explain how the paradigm of the interviewer is important in conducting a clinical interview.

4.   In measuring stress, how is the Assessment of Daily Experience an improvement over the Social Readjustment Rating Scale?

5.   How was the MMPI developed?

6.   Describe the rationale underlying Exner's scoring system for the Rorschach.

7.   How valid are IQ tests? Explain briefly.

8.   What is done in ecological momentary assessment?

9.   What are the problems in studying neurotransmitters in psychopathology?

10.   How do neuropsychological tests provide information about brain functioning?

Internet Resources

The following are Internet resources to begin exploring the topics in this chapter. Additional general Internet resources are at the end of the introduction chapter.

BehaveNet Clinical Capsules has criteria for the DSM-IV TR diagnostic categories.

www.behavenet.com/capsules/disorders/dsm4TRclassification.htm

Internet Mental Health has information on a wide range of psychological problems.

www.mentalhealth.com

Answers to Self-Test, Chapter 3

Multiple Choice

1. b (p. 62)	2. b (p. 64-65)	3. c (p. 67)	4. b (p. 71-72)
5. c (p. 72)	6. a (p. 73)	7. a (p. 78)	8. c (p. 80)
9. a (p. 85-86)	10. d (p. 97)		

Short Answer

1. By showing that people with and without the label differ on a variety of measures. For example, he could collect data showing that they differ in self-reports, reports of others, physiological measures, background, prognosis, response to treatment, etc. (p. 63)

2. Examples in which people differ in the *amount or quantity of* some characteristic. For example; height, weight, grade point average, intelligence, or income. (p. 72)

3. Interviewer's paradigm influences what information the interviewer seeks, how the interviewer acts (asking questions vs. listening, etc.), and interprets what the interviewee says. (p. 75)

4. The Assessment of Daily Experience has the person rate his/her stress every day avoiding the problems of memory and retrospective reports in the Social Readjustment Rating Scale. (p. 78)

5. Initially, clinicians suggested items. The items were given to people with and without various diagnoses. Those items that distinguished particular diagnoses were used in the final test. (p. 79-80)

6. It assumes that a person's responses to the Rorschach use the same cognitive and perceptual patterns used in responding to real-life situations. For example, a person who focuses on dark features of the inkblots may also focus on dark, gloomy aspects of life. (p. 82)

7. They have good criterion validity in that they predict academic, occupational, etc. success. However, they only measure what psychologists consider intelligence. Other factors are important in success, including motivation, family background, and school anxiety. (p. 85)

8. People are asked to collect data in real time. For example, a timer might remind them to rate their stress level every two hours. (p. 86)

9. We can only measure their byproducts (in blood and urine) which could have come from neurotransmitters anywhere in the body. The differences show only a correlation (did the neurotransmitter change cause the disorder or vice versa?). (p. 91-92)

10. They use a variety of measures designed to rely on different, specific areas of the brain. Doing poorly on one measure suggests a deficit in that area of the brain. (p. 93)

4 Research Methods in the Study of Psychopathology

Overview

This is the last of four introductory chapters covering basic issues in psychopathology. The first two chapters covered historical and contemporary paradigms or theories of psychopathology. Chapter 3 dealt with DSM-IV-TR, the current standard system of classification, and then went on to summarize current assessment methods.

Chapter 4 discusses research methods and will complete the introductory chapters. Research issues have been mentioned in earlier chapters and will appear throughout the text. Chapter 4 brings these issues into focus by directly comparing the methods and limits of various research approaches.

Chapter 5 begins eleven chapters covering the various forms of psychopathology. Chapters 5, 6, and 7 will discuss various disorders directly or indirectly related to anxiety and stress.

Chapter Summary

Science and Scientific Methods   Science involves forming a theory and then systematically gathering data to test the theory. It is important for researchers to replicate findings from a given study.

Approaches to Research on Psychopathology   Common methods for studying abnormal behavior include case studies, correlational studies, and experimental studies. Each method has strengths and weaknesses.

Clinical case studies provide detailed descriptions of rare or unusual phenomena or novel procedures. Case studies can disconfirm that a relationship is universal and can generate hypotheses that can be tested through controlled research. Case studies, however, may not always be valid, and they are of limited value in providing evidence to support a theory.

Correlational methods are the most common way to study the causes of abnormal behavior, because we can not manipulate diagnoses or most of the key risk variables that we believe cause disease.

Conclusions drawn from correlational studies cannot be interpreted in cause-effect terms because of the directionality. Longitudinal studies help address which variable came first, but can still suffer from the third-variable problems.

One form of correlational study, epidemiological research, involves gathering information about the prevalence and incidence of disorders in populations and about risk factors that relate to higher probability of developing a disorder. Epidemiological studies avoid the sampling biases seen in studies of people drawn from undergraduate psychology classes or from treatment clinics.

Studies of behavioral genetics often rely on correlational techniques as well. The most common behavioral genetic methods include the family method, the twin method, and the adoptees method.

In the experimental method, the researcher randomly assigns people to an experimental group or a control group. Effects of the independent variable, or experimental condition, on a dependent variable are then tested. Treatment studies are a common example of experimental research, although some controversy has arisen about the use of placebos. Many different forms of analogue studies are conducted in psychopathology research. Single case experimental designs can provide well-controlled data.

Generally, experimental methods help enhance internal validity, but correlational methods sometimes offer greater external validity.

Integrating the Findings of Multiple Studies   Meta-analysis is an important tool for reaching general conclusions from a group of research studies. It entails putting the result of statistical comparisons into a common format—the effect size—so the results of many studies can be averaged.

Learning Goals

1.   Be able to define science and the scientific method.

2.   Be able to describe the advantages and disadvantages of correlational and experimental designs.

3.   Be able to identify common types of correlational and experimental designs.

4.   Be able to describe the basic steps in conducting a meta-analysis.

Key Terms

Theory (p. 100)

Hypothesis (p. 100)

Case study (p. 102)

Correlational method (p. 105)

Correlation (p. 105)

Correlation coefficient (p. 106)

Statistical significance (p. 106)

Clinical significance (p. 107)

Directionality problem (p. 108)

Longitudinal design (p. 108)

Cross-sectional design (p. 108)

High-risk method (p. 108)

Third-variable problem (p. 108)

Epidemiology (p. 108)

Prevalence (p. 108)

Incidence (p. 108)

Risk factors (p. 108)

Family method (p. 109)

Index cases [probands] (p. 110)

Twin method (p. 110)

Monozygotic [MZ] twins (p. 110)

Dizygotic [DZ] twins (p. 110)

Concordance (p. 110)

Adoptees method (p. 110)

Cross-fostering (p. 110)

The experiment (p. 111)

Random assignment (p. 111)

Independent variable (p. 111)

Dependent variable (p. 111)

Experimental effect (p. 112)

Internal validity (p. 112)

Control group (p. 113)

Placebo (p. 113)

External validity (p. 113)

Double-blind procedure (p. 114)

Analogue experiment (p. 115)

Single-subject experimental design (p. 116)

Reversal [ABAB] design (p. 116)

Meta-analysis (p. 118)

Study Questions

Science and Scientific Methods (p. 100-102)

1.   Describe the role of theories and hypotheses in science. How are they related? (p. 100-102)

Approaches to Research on Psychopathology (p. 102-117)

2.   What are case studies? Explain the limitation and three uses of case studies. (p. 102-105)

3.   What are correlational methods and how are they different from experimental research? How are correlations measured?   How are correlation coefficients understood? What does it mean to say that a correlation is statistically significant and is clinically significant? (p. 105-107)

4.   Describe two problems of causality in correlational methods. How are longitudinal designs and high risk studies used to try to overcome the first of these problems? (p. 107-108)

5.   As an example of correlational methods, describe epidemiology. Why is representativeness critical to epidemiological studies? (p. 108-109)

6.   As another example of correlational methods, describe three methods of behavior genetics. How are data from the first two interpreted and what third variable problems complicate interpretation? (p. 109-110)

7.   Explain the four basic features of an experiment. What is internal validity? Describe how control groups and random assignments are used to eliminate confounds and provide internal validity. (p. 112-113)

8.   What is external validity, and what are some reasons it is difficult to demonstrate? What are analogue experiments? What are an advantage and a disadvantage of using analogues in experimental designs?   Explain how various kinds of studies can complement each other to increase external validity. (p. 113-116)

9.   What are single-subject designs generally? What is the ABAB design, and how does it show that the manipulation produced the result? What is the primary disadvantage of this design? What is the disadvantage of single-subject designs generally? (p. 116-117)

Integrating the Findings of Multiple Studies (p. 118-119)

10.   Explain why it is typically necessary to integrate the findings of multiple studies. What is meta-analysis, and how can it help? What is a common problem in meta-analyses? (p. 118-119)

Self-Test, Chapter 4

(* Items not covered in Study Questions.)

Multiple Choice

1. Scientific theories are judged by how well they
    a. relate to the world outside the laboratory.
    b. explain the data.
    c. compare to other theories.
    d. can be tested.

2. A difficulty of case studies is
    a. lack of objectivity.
    b. limited control.
    c. few cases for comparison.
    d. all of the above choices are correct.

3. If a researcher obtained a negative correlation between a measure of anxiety and a measure of test performance, this would mean that as anxiety goes up, test scores
    a. go up.
    b. go down.
    c. are unaffected.
    d. sometimes go up and sometimes go down.

4. To deal with the problem of statistically significant correlations in very large samples, researchers also attend to whether the correlation
    a. is large enough to be of clinical significance.
    b. is above .85.
    c. is negative or positive.
    d. is the same if you make the sample smaller.

* 5. What is an inherent problem with longitudinal designs?
    a. They cannot provide causation data.
    b. They are often prohibitively expensive and provide little data.
    c. Causes and effects are measured at the same point in time.
    d. They fail to address the directionality problem.

* 6. Prevalence refers to
    a. the likelihood that a disorder will be found in another culture.
    b. the proportion of a population that has a disorder now.
    c. the number of people who contract a disorder in a given time period.
    d. the likelihood that a person will have a disorder given that they have a particular characteristic.

7. Determining the influence of being raised by disordered parents and eliminating that influence in behavior genetics research is accomplished by the _____ method
    a. twin
    b. adoptees
    c. family
    d. spouse

8.   In order to be certain that the effects are due to the experimental manipulation, experimenters typically include
       a. more participants.
       b. a control group.
       c. a different experimental group.
       d. a diverse group of participants.

9.   External validity is demonstrated by
       a. repetition in different situations.
       b. analogue experiments.
       c. random assignment to control groups.
       d. double-blind procedures.

10.   One of the main criticisms of meta-analysis is
       a. there is no way to standardize differences between groups from various studies.
       b. researchers include studies that are of poor quality.
       c. the literature search required for meta-analysis is prohibitively extensive.
       d. effect size is not a reliable statistic.

Short Answer

1.   What is the difference between a correlational study and an experiment?

2.   Professor Smith reports that mature students get better grades based on his study showing tha college seniors have higher grade point averages than freshmen, however, you disagree. Wha is the term for Professor Smith's error? Explain.

3.   In epidemiological studies, why is representativeness important?

4.   Describe what is done in the adoptees method.

5.   Experiments are said to be internally valid if . . .

6.   What does it mean to say that random assignment eliminates confounds?

7.   Why is it difficult to demonstrate external validity?

8.   You hypothesize that your professor tells jokes in class because you laugh at them. Design a single-subject ABAB design to test your hypothesis.

9.   What is the disadvantage of single-subject designs generally? Explain.

10.   Why is meta-analysis needed?

Internet Resources

The following are Internet resources to begin exploring the topics in this chapter. Additional general Internet resources are at the end of the introduction chapter.

American Psychological Society is a major association of research-oriented psychologists with links to many related sites.   www.psychologicalscience.org

The Many Faces of Psychological Research in the 21st Century is an on-line text published by the Society for the Teaching of Psychology.   teachpsych.lemoyne.edu/teachpsych/faces/facesindex.html

Using Meta-analysis to Evaluate Evidence: Practical Tips and Traps discusses techniques and issues in doing meta-analysis.   www.cpa-apc.org/Publications/Archives/CJP/2005/march/Lam.asp

Answers to Self-Test, Chapter 4

Multiple Choice

1. d (p. 102)	2. d (p. 102)	3. b (p. 106)	4. a (p. 107)
5. b (p. 108)	6. b (p. 108)	7. b (p. 110)	8. b (p. 112-113)
9. a (p. 113)	10. b (p. 118)		

Short Answer

1. Correlational studies measure, but do not manipulate, variables. Experiments manipulate variables. (p. 105)

2. Professor Smith forgot about the directionality problem. It's possible that seniors get better grades because they're mature. It's also possible that faculty grade senior classes more leniently. (You can, surely, think of additional possibilities.) (p. 108)

3. The people studied need to be representative of the larger group on important variables or the results will not generalize to the group. (p. 109)

4. This method looks at children who were adopted and raised apart from their biological parents. If they have the same chrematistics as their biological parents, this suggests a genetic factor. (p. 110)

5. The effect can be confidently attributed to manipulating the independent variable. (p. 112)

6. By randomly assigning participants to groups any individual characteristics of the participants which might influence the results (i.e. be confounds) are equally likely to occur in all groups. (p. 113)

7. There is no way to know for sure that something about another situation might affect the results. The best one can do is perform similar experiments in new situations. (p. 113)

8. Laugh at each joke your professor tells for one class session and don't laugh for the next session. Repeat this several times. Count the number of jokes told in each session. (p. 116)

9. The disadvantage is external validity. That is, it's hard to prove the results will generalize to other subjects. (p. 117)

10. Meta-analysis provides a systematic way to compare large numbers of similar studies. (p. 118)

5 Anxiety Disorders

Overview

The first four chapters have discussed a number of basic ideas and issues in abnormal psychology. These concepts provide a framework for surveying the various forms of abnormality. You will want to refer back to those chapters periodically as you study the rest of the text.

The next eleven chapters survey the various forms of psychopathology. Now would be a good time to glance over all these chapters. Notice that they cover a wide range of problem behaviors. A number of them are matters of current social debate. After covering forms of psychopathology, the last two chapters in the text discuss issues in psychological treatment as well as legal and ethical issues.

Chapters 5 through 7 discuss problems related, in various ways, to anxiety and stress. Chapter 5 covers anxiety disorders such as phobias and panic disorder. These more or less directly involve excessive fears, worries, and anxiety. Chapter 6 discusses two groups of problems in which anxiety may be more subtly involved. They are somatoform disorders, characterized by physical symptoms or complaints, and dissociative disorders, involving disturbances in memory and awareness. Although the traditional psychoanalytic term "neurosis" is no longer used to describe these problems, anxiety is still seen as involved in various ways. Finally, Chapter 7 deals with the role of stress and anxiety in physical health and problems (for example, heart problems and asthma).

Chapter Summary

Clinical Descriptions of the Anxiety Disorders As a class, anxiety disorders are the most common type of mental illness.

DSM-IV-TR lists seven principal diagnoses: specific phobia, social phobia, panic disorder (with and without agoraphobia), generalized anxiety disorder, obsessive-compulsive disorder, posttraumatic stress disorder, and acute stress disorder. Anxiety is common to all the anxiety disorders, but phobias and panic also involve fear as a clinical feature.

Phobias are intense, unreasonable fears that interfere with functioning. Social phobia is fear of unknown people or social scrutiny. Specific phobias include fears of animals, heights, enclosed spaces, and blood, injury, or injections.

A patient with panic disorder has recurrent, inexplicable attacks of intense fear. Panic attacks alone are not sufficient for the diagnosis; a person must be worried about the potential of having another attack. Panic attacks sometimes lead to fear and avoidance of being in places where escape would be difficult if another attack were to occur, known as agoraphobia.

In generalized anxiety disorder, the person is beset with virtually constant tension, apprehension, and worry which last for at least 6 months.

People with obsessive-compulsive disorder have intrusive, unwanted thoughts and feel pressured to engage in rituals to avoid overwhelming levels of anxiety.

Posttraumatic stress disorder is diagnosed in some people who have experienced a traumatic event that would evoke extreme distress in most people. It is marked by symptoms of reexperiencing the trauma, arousal, and emotional numbing. Acute stress disorder is defined by similar symptoms, but lasts less than one month.

Gender and Sociocultural Factors in the Anxiety Disorders Anxiety disorders are much more common among women than men.

The focus of anxiety, the prevalence of anxiety disorders, and the specific symptoms expressed may be shaped by culture.

Common Risk Factors across the Anxiety Disorders The psychoanalytic view of anxiety disorders is that they are a defense against repressed conflicts.

Genes increase risk for a broad range of anxiety disorders. Beyond this general risk for anxiety disorders, there may be more specific heritability for certain anxiety disorders.

Beyond genetic diatheses, other factors that appear to be involved in a range of anxiety disorders include elevated activity in the fear circuit, poor regulation of several neurotransmitter systems (GABA, serotonin, and norepinephrine), lack of perceived control, a tendency to pay closer attention to signs of potential danger, and negative life events.

Common Aspects of Treatment for the Anxiety Disorders Behavior therapists focus on exposure to what is feared. Systematic desensitization and modeling may be used as parts of exposure therapy. For some disorders, including social phobia, GAD, OCD and panic disorder, cognitive components may also be helpful in therapy.

Antidepressants and benzodiazapenes are most commonly used for anxiety disorders, but new research also has begun to focus on medications like the anticonvulsant medication, gabapentin (Neurontin). The effects of medications are often not as powerful as those seen for psychotherapy. There are some concerns that benzodiazapenes are subject to abuse, and discontinuing medications usually leads to relapse.

Etiology and Treatment of Specific Anxiety Disorders Behavioral models of phobias typically emphasize two stages of conditioning. The first stage involves classical conditioning, in which a formerly innocuous object is paired with a feared object. This could be accomplished through direct exposure, modeling, or cognition. Fears of objects with evolutionary significance may be more easily conditioned. The second stage involves avoidance. Because not all people with negative experiences develop phobias, diatheses must be important. Exposure treatment for specific phobia tends to work quickly and well. Social phobia is harder to treat and adding cognitive components to behavioral treatments may help.

Neurobiological models of panic disorder have focused on the locus ceruleus, the brain center responsible for norepinephrine release. Many different drugs have been found to trigger panic attacks in laboratory studies among people with a history of panic attacks. The key trigger is probably not a shift in a given neurotransmitter, but rather, how a person interprets changes in his/her body. Behavioral theories of panic attacks have posited that the attacks are classically conditioned to internal bodily sensations. Cognitive theories suggest that such sensations are more frightening due to catastrophic misinterpretation of somatic cues. CBT treatment appears more effective than medication treatment of panic disorder.

Cognitive behavioral theories hold that GAD results from distorted cognitive processes. One model suggests that worry actually helps people avoid more intense emotions. Neurobiological approaches focus on the neurotransmitter, GABA, which may be deficient in those with the disorder. Relaxation and cognitive approaches may be helpful, as well as medication approaches.

OCD symptoms have been robustly linked to activity in the orbitofrontal cortex, the caudate, and the anterior cingulate. In behavioral accounts, compulsions are considered avoidance responses that are reinforced because they provide relief. Checking behaviors may be intensified by doubts about memories. Obsessions may be intensified by attempts to inhibit unwanted thoughts, in part because people with OCD seem to feel that thinking about something is as bad as doing it. ERP is a well-validated approach that involves exposure. The SSRI, clomipramine, also appears helpful, as do other antidepressant medications.

Research and theory on the causes of posttraumatic stress disorder focus on risk factors such as hippocampal volume, the severity of the event, dissociation, and other psychological factors that may influence the ability to cope with stress, such as social support and intelligence. Psychological treatment involves exposure; often imaginal exposure.

To My Students

This is the first of many chapters covering specific psychological disorders. As you study them, you will discover that each follows the same general outline. First, the problem is defined and any issues regarding its classification in DSM-IV-TR are discussed. Second, theories and research into its causes are described. Finally, various treatments are summarized. Of course the outline varies, but you will find it helpful to look for this kind of outline as you study each chapter and to organize your studying around it.

This is also a good time to warn you of a common experience among students studying abnormal psychology. Often, students in these courses come to believe they may have the problem covered in each chapter. For example, you may think you have an anxiety disorder when studying Chapter 5, depression in Chapter 8, and schizophrenia in Chapter 11. If this happens to you, don't be surprised. The various problems covered in the text are exaggerations of very normal tendencies in all of us. If you can see these tendencies in yourself, it probably means you have developed a meaningful understanding of the problem. Of course, if you are seriously concerned, you can discuss the matter with your instructor or someone at your school's counseling center. They are used to such situations, and you may be surprised at how easily they understand your concerns.

Learning Goals

1. Be able to describe the clinical features of the anxiety disorders, and how they tend to co-occur with each other.

2. Be able to describe how gender and culture influence the prevalence of anxiety disorders.

3. Be able to recognize commonalities in etiology and treatment across the anxiety disorders.

4. Be able to describe etiological factors and treatment approaches that are specific to each of the anxiety disorders.

Key Terms

Anxiety (p. 122)

Fear (p. 122)

Anxiety disorders (p. 122)

Phobia (p. 123)

Specific phobia (p. 123)

Comorbidity (p. 123)

Social phobia (p. 124)

Panic disorder (p. 125)

Panic attack (p. 125)

Depersonalization (p. 125)

Derealization (p. 125)

Agoraphobia (p. 126)

Generalized anxiety disorder [GAD] (p. 126)

Obsessive-compulsive disorder [OCD] (p. 127)

Obsessions (p. 127)

Compulsions (p. 127-128)

Posttraumatic stress disorder [PTSD] (p. 129)

Acute stress disorder (p. 130)

Subthreshold symptoms (p. 130)

Fear circuit (p. 133)

Neuroses (p. 134)

Behavioral inhibition (p. 134)

Neuroticism (p. 134)

Anxiolytics (p. 136)

Benzodiazepines (p. 136)

Antidepressants (p. 136)

Tricyclic antidepressants (p. 136)

Selective serotonin reuptake inhibitor [SSRI] (p. 136)

Mowrer's two-factor model (p. 138-139)

Prepared learning (p. 140)

Beta blockers (p. 142)

Locus ceruleus (p. 143)

Interoceptive conditioning (p. 144)

Anxiety Sensitivity Index (p. 145)

Fear-of-fear hypothesis (p. 145)

Panic control therapy (p. 145)

Orbitofrontal cortex (p. 148)

Anterior cingulate (p. 148)

Thought suppression (p. 149)

Exposure and ritual prevention (p. 150)

Nonverbal memories (p. 152)

Dissociation (p. 153)

Imaginal exposure (p. 154)

Eye movement desensitization and reprocessing (p. 154)

Critical incident stress debriefing (p. 155)

Study Questions

Clinical Descriptions of the Anxiety Disorders (p. 122-131)

1.   The text describes five anxiety disorders. For each disorder describe a) its symptoms or characteristics, b) any sub-types, c) how it is distinguished from similar normal behaviors. (Note that agoraphobia, one of the phobias, is discussed with panic disorder. Why?) (p. 122-130)

2.   How common is comorbidity in anxiety disorders? Give several reasons for comorbidity with other anxiety disorders and with other disorders (beside anxiety disorders). (p. 130-131)

Gender and Sociocultural Factors in the Anxiety Disorders (p. 131-132)

3.   Describe gender differences in anxiety disorders and two possible explanations. Describe two cultural differences in anxiety disorders with possible explanations as well as research suggesting that cultural differences may be artifacts. (p. 131-132)

Common Risk Factors across the Anxiety Disorders (p. 133-136)

4.   How strong is the heritability of anxiety disorders? Describe two lines of evidence suggesting a neurobiological factor in anxiety disorders. Describe two lines of evidence suggesting that personality traits contribute to anxiety disorders. (p. 133-134)

5. What cognitive belief pattern is common in people with anxiety disorders? What two factors may maintain this belief?   What environmental events may contribute to anxiety disorders? (p. 134-136)

Common Aspects of Treatments for the Anxiety Disorders (p. 136-137)

6. Describe the common emphasis in psychological treatment for anxiety disorders. Identify two kinds of medications commonly used and two common problems with them. (p. 136-137)

Etiology and Treatment of Specific Anxiety Disorders (p. 138-155)

7. Describe Mowrer's two-factor model of the etiology of specific phobias.   Describe two extensions of it and a biological implication. Describe how the two-factor model is adapted for social phobias. What cognitive factors also appear to be common? (p. 138-141)

8. Describe how exposure is adapted in the treatment of specific phobias and social phobias. Describe the use of cognitive therapy and medication for specific phobias and social phobias. What is the effect of combining medications with psychological treatment? (p. 141-143)

9. In the etiology of panic disorder, describe animal research on the role of the locus ceruleus and human research on triggering panic attacks. What giant puzzle exists and what does this suggest about the role of cognitions? From a behavioral view, describe interoceptive conditioning as a way of understanding this process. From a cognitive view, describe two factors suggested by research and research indicating these cognitive factors precede the start of panic attacks. How have these ideas been extended to agoraphobia? (p. 143-145)

10. As a treatment for panic disorder, describe panic control therapy and results of research comparing its effectiveness to drugs. Summarize the general approach and effectiveness of treatment for panic disorders with agoraphobia. Why are medications often used to treat panic disorder and what are their limits? (p. 145-146)

11.   Summarize cognitive factors in generalized anxiety disorder (GAD).   How effective are treatments for GAD generally? Describe two behavioral and cognitive approaches to treatment. How effective are medications overall? (p. 147-148)

12.   Regarding obsessive-compulsive disorder (OCD), how has research identified brain areas involved, and why is it unclear that these areas cause OCD? Summarize three behavioral and cognitive ideas on causes of OCD. Describe the behavioral approach to treating OCD and its effectiveness.   How do cognitive therapists modify this approach?   How effective are medications for OCD? (p. 148-151)

13.   For posttraumatic stress disorder (PTSD), what has research shown about the nature of the trauma and two neurobiological factors?   Describe one behavioral and two psychological factors in the etiology of PTSD. Describe exposure treatment for PTSD. How effective is it, and why is it difficult?   How effective are medications for PTSD? Why is treatment of acute stress disorder important? (p. 151-155)

Self-Test, Chapter 5

(* Items not covered in Study Questions.)

Multiple Choice

* 1.   Fear is adaptive in that
    a. it prepares the body for escape or fighting.
    b. it prepares the body for future threats.
    c. it involves very moderate levels of arousal.
    d. all of the above are true.

2.   Pasquale is fearful of heights and flying, which has hampered his career. According to DSM-IV-TR, his condition would be diagnosed as
    a. agoraphobia.
    b. panic disorder.
    c. specific phobia.
    d. posttraumatic stress disorder.

3.   Hilda reports that she feels like she is outside of her body. Which of the following symptoms is she describing?
    a. flashbacks
    b. exogenous perception
    c. derealization
    d. depersonalization

4.   Most compulsions are viewed as _____ by the person performing them.
    a. pleasurable
    b. rational
    c. absurd
    d. anxiety provoking

5.   New research on cultural differences in expression of symptoms suggests that
    a. collectivist cultures more commonly express physical symptoms of anxiety.
    b. across cultures, people tend to underemphasize somatic concerns of anxiety.
    c. the ratio of somatic to psychological symptoms in anxiety is quite similar across cultures.
    d. medical clinics are a better place to study anxiety.

* 6.   Which of the following is a reason for the lack of treatment-seeking by individuals with anxiety disorder?
    a. Individuals with anxiety disorders are often too neurotic to seek treatment.
    b. Individuals with anxiety disorders are often in denial.
    c. Individuals with anxiety disorders do not perceive that they have a problem.
    d. Anxiety disorders are among the least serious of psychological disorders.

7.   Jim was bitten by a goose when he was a child. Now, as an adult, when he goes to ponds where geese flock, he experiences fear and leaves. His anxiety subsides once he leaves. This illustrates the _____ theory of phobias.

    a. two-factor
    b. psychoanalytic
    c. learning
    d. cognitive

8.   Panic Control Therapy (PCT) has been found
      a. to be no better than medication, either immediately after treatment or at follow-up.
      b. to have the same effect as medication, but was superior at follow-up.
      c. to have a significantly higher effect at the end of treatment and at follow-up.
      d. to be inferior to medication.

9.   Which of the following is not generally used as a treatment for GAD?
      a. antidepressants
      b. relaxation training
      c. challenging the person's thoughts
      d. exposure

10.   Which of the following is considered to be most effective in treating PTSD?
      a. medication
      b. social support
      c. supportive psychotherapy
      d. exposure to trauma-related events

Short Answer

1.   Why is agoraphobia commonly discussed with panic disorder?

2.   Why do people with anxiety disorders often also have other psychological disorders?

3   Describe two kinds of research suggesting a neurobiological factor in anxiety disorders.

4.   What cognitive belief is common in people with anxiety disorders? Explain briefly.

5.   Describe the common theme in psychological treatment of all anxiety disorders.

6.   Mary is chronically anxious. She is very shy and awkward around others and avoids social contact much of the time. She reports feeling that she can't do anything right and that no one likes her. How would a cognitive behavioral therapist view her problem?

7.   Describe what is done in systematic desensitization as a treatment for phobias.

8.   Describe the fear-of-fear hypothesis as part of the etiology of agoraphobia.

9.   Describe the common behavioral approach to the treatment of compulsions and its effectiveness.

10.   Briefly describe two psychological factors that influence whether people exposed to trauma will develop PTSD.

Internet Resources

The following are Internet resources to begin exploring the topics in this chapter. Additional general Internet resources are at the end of the introduction chapter.

Anxiety Disorders Association of America (ADAA) offers information on understanding and treating anxiety disorders for consumers.   www.adaa.org

Anxiety and Panic: Gaining Control Over How You're Feeling provides suggestions for managing anxiety.   familydoctor.org/013.xml

Gift from Within for survivors of trauma and victimization offers online resources and links to support groups.   www.giftfromwithin.org

National Center for PTSD is sponsored by the Department of Veterans Affairs and has a lot of information on PTSD in the military.   www.ncptsd.org

Obsessive-compulsive foundation (OCF) offers consumer-oriented information on OCD including research, training, and support groups.   www.ocfoundation.org

Treatment of Posttraumatic Stress Disorder Expert Consensus Guidelines offers consensus suggestions for treatment and for victims of PTSD and their families.
                                                psychguides.com/gl-treatment_of_PTSD.html

Answers to Self-Test, Chapter 5

Multiple Choice

1. a (p. 122)   2. c (p. 123)   3. d (p. 125)   4. c (p. 128)
5. c (p. 132)   6. c (p. 136)   7. a (p. 138)   8. b (p. 146)
9. d (p. 147-148)   10. d (p. 153)

Short Answer

1.   Because panic attacks often lead to agoraphobia. The person comes to fear and avoid public places (agoraphobia) for fear of having a panic attack in them. (p. 126)

2.   Because prolonged anxiety often leads to other problems. People with prolonged anxiety may become exhausted and depressed, abuse substances to reduce anxiety, or become socially limited (several personality disorders). (p. 130-131)

3.   The fear circuit, especially the amygdala, is more activated in people with anxiety who are shown sad/angry faces. Neurotransmitters involved in the fear circuit, especially serotonin and GABA, appear to function poorly. (p. 133-134)

4.   They tend to fear that bad things will happen. They fear they cannot control these bad things and attend to and remember any bad things that do happen to them. (p. 134-135)

5.   Common theme is exposure. The person must be helped to face his/her fears and his/her beliefs about them. (p. 136)

6.   Therapist would see her anxiety as tied to social fears (a social phobia). (p. 141)

7.   The individual is taught how to relax deeply. Then, while relaxed, the person is exposed (perhaps in imagination) to a series of gradually more fearful situations. (p. 141)

8.   Hypothesis that they are terrified of becoming afraid in public places. They fear that terrible consequences will follow if they become or appear afraid in a public place. (p. 145)

9.   Exposure and response prevention in which the person experiences a situation that would, normally, result in a compulsive action without doing it. The approach is only modestly effective resulting in only partial improvement for most people. (p. 150)

10.   People are less likely to develop PTSD if they had or felt some degree of control during the trauma and if they cope by talking about it to friends. People who avoid thinking/talking about their trauma are more likely to develop PTSD. (p. 153)

6 Somatoform Disorders And Dissociative Disorders

Overview

Chapter 6 is the second of three chapters on disorders related to anxiety and stress. The previous chapter discussed disorders involving fairly direct expressions of anxiety. They included chronic anxiety, phobias or unreasonable fears, and obsessions and compulsions in which people think and do things in order to control anxiety. Chapter 6 covers two groups of disorders in which people do not complain of anxiety or stress, but anxiety and stress are still believed to be involved. The two groups are somatoform disorders (involving physical complaints) and dissociative disorders (involving altered memory and awareness). Both arise from psychological factors such as anxiety and stress.

After this, Chapter 7 discusses how anxiety and stress are involved in physical health and illness. Traditionally, we have recognized the role of stress in psychophysiological disorders such as asthma and heart conditions. However, we now recognize that stress can play a role in all physical/medical problems. You might note that somatoform disorders (in Chapter 6) involve physical complaints, while the problems in Chapter 7 involve physical tissue changes (not just complaints).

Chapter Summary

Somatoform Disorders In somatoform disorders, biological explanations for physical symptoms cannot be found. The major somatoform diagnoses include pain disorder, body dysmorphic disorder, hypochondriasis, conversion disorder, and somatization disorder.

Psychoanalytic theory proposes that in conversion disorder, repressed impulses are converted into physical symptoms. Cultural factors influencing how people think about and express distress may play a role in the disorder as well.

Data regarding other somatoform disorder are less available; somatoform disorders do not appear to be inherited in general. There may be some neurobiological overlap between body dysmorphic disorder and obsessive compulsive disorder. Cognitive behavioral models emphasize that some people may have a cognitive style that leads them to overly attend to physical symptoms or problems and to make negative attributions about these symptoms and their implications. The form of the cognitive bias may differ for the various somatoform disorders. Behavioral reinforcement may maintain help-seeking behavior.

Antidepressants have been shown to be effective for some somatoform disorders. In psychoanalytic treatments for somatoform disorders, analysts try to help the client face the repressed impulses. Cognitive behavioral treatments, which have received a great deal of support, try to address the maladaptive negative cognitions about physical symptoms, to reduce anxiety, and to reinforce behavior that is not consistent with the sick role.

Dissociative Disorders Dissociative disorders are defined by disruptions of consciousness, memory, and identity.

The dissociative disorders include dissociative amnesia, dissociative fugue, depersonalization disorder, and dissociative identity disorder.

Most of the writing about the causes of dissociative disorders focuses on dissociative identity disorder. Psychoanalytic theory regards dissociative disorders as instances of massive repression of some undesirable event or aspect of the self. People with dissociative identity disorder very often report severe physical or sexual abuse during childhood. One model, the posttraumatic model, suggests that extensive reliance on dissociation to fend off overwhelming feelings from abuse puts people at risk for developing dissociative identity disorder. The sociocognitive model, though, raises the question of whether some of these symptoms are elicited by treatment. Proponents of the sociocognitive model point out that abuse in childhood may result in high levels of suggestibility, that some therapists use strategies that suggest such symptoms to people, and that most people do not recognize the presence of any alters until after they see a therapist.

Regardless of theoretical orientation, all clinicians focus their treatment efforts on helping the person cope with anxiety, face fears more directly, and operate in a manner that integrates his/her memory and consciousness.

Psychoanalytic treatment is perhaps the most commonly used treatment for dissociative disorders, but some of the techniques involved, such as hypnosis and an attempt to unbury memories, may make symptoms worse.

Learning Goals

1.   Be able to define the symptoms of the somatoform and dissociative disorders.

2.   Be able to explain the psychoanalytic and sociocultural perspectives on conversion disorder.

3.   Be able to discuss neurobiological and cognitive behavioral models of other somatoform disorders.

4.   Be able to summarize current debate regarding the etiology of dissociative identity disorders.

5.   Be able to describe the goals and issues in available treatments for somatoform and dissociative disorders.

Key Terms

Somatoform disorders (p. 159)

Pain disorder (p. 159-160)

Malingering (p. 160)

La belle indifference (p. 160)

Factitious disorder (p. 160)

Body dysmorphic disorder (p. 161)

Hypochondriasis (p. 162)

Somatization disorder (p. 162)

Conversion disorder (p. 164)

Anesthesia (p. 164)

Blindsight (p. 167)

Dissociative disorders (p. 173)

Dissociation (p. 174)

Dissociative amnesia (p. 175)

Explicit memory (p. 177)

Implicit memory (p. 177)

Dissociative fugue (p. 178)

Depersonalization disorder (p. 178)

Dissociative identity disorder [DID] (p. 179)

Posttraumatic model (p. 182)

Sociogenic model (p. 182)

Study Questions

Somatoform Disorders (p. 159-173)

1.   What are the general characteristics of somatoform disorders? Describe and distinguish among four types of somatoform disorders (which are not discussed in detail). (p. 159-164)

2.   Give some examples of conversion symptoms involving loss of (a) motor and (b) sensory functioning. Why is it difficult, but important, to distinguish between conversions and medical conditions? (p. 164-165)

3.   Explain why conversion disorder occupies a central place in psychoanalytic theory. Summarize Freud's theory and how contemporary research led to a revision. Summarize research on genetic and cultural factors in conversion disorders. (p. 166-168)

4. Summarize research on the etiology of the other somatoform disorders, including genetic and neurobiological factors. From a behavioral-cognitive perspective, how might these disorders develop? (p. 168-170)

5. Why has little research been done on the psychological treatment of somatoform disorders? Describe the general techniques used by cognitive-behavioral therapists in treating somatoform disorders. (p. 170)

6. How do therapists approach pain disorder, body dysmorphic disorder, hypocondriasis, somatization disorder, and conversion disorder? (p. 171-173)

Dissociative Disorders (p. 173-186)

7.   Describe normal dissociation. What is the presumed basis for dissociative disorders, and why is little known about them? What does research suggest about memory of stressful events and about dissociation? (p. 174-175)

8.   Define and distinguish among four dissociative disorders. (p. 175-181). Identify two reasons that dissociative identity disorder (DID) is confusing and controversial (p. 181).

9.   How has the incidence of DID changed over time? Describe two theories of DID that developed, in part, out of the changes in incidence. Summarize four kinds of evidence regarding this issue. (p. 181-184)

10. In psychoanalytic treatment of DID, what is the general goal and common method? Why is research limited, and what has been reported? (p. 184-186)

Self-Test, Chapter 6

(* Items not covered in Study Questions.)

Multiple Choice

* 1.   Given the excessive preoccupation with a perceived bodily imperfection, body dysmorphic disorder has been considered most similar to which disorder?
     a. specific phobia
     b. obsessive-compulsive disorder
     c. social phobia
     d. conversion disorder

2.   Most conversion symptoms suggest
     a. loss of memory.
     b. damage to the uterus.
     c. renal dysfunction.
     d. neurological damage.

3.   The psychoanalytic concept of _____ is based upon Freud's study of conversion disorder.
     a. libido
     b. hysteria
     c. the Oedipal complex
     d. the unconscious

4.   Social and cultural factors in conversion disorder are suggested by data indicating that conversion disorder
     a. has been occurring less frequently over the past century.
     b. is most prevalent in urban centers.
     c. is more common in societies with greater sexual freedom.
     d. is most prevalent in formerly communist countries.

5.   Research on the treatment of somatoform disorders indicates
     a. that no treatment is effective for very long as most patients relapse.
     b. that psychoanalytic treatments are superior.
     c. that behavioral treatments are most effective.
     d. none of the above; little research has been done on treatment of somatoform disorders.

6.   Megan is currently in treatment for hypochondriasis. Her psychologist employs a cognitive-behavioral approach. Which of the following is Megan's psychologist least likely to do?
     a. help Megan to think in less pessimistic ways
     b. point out Megan's extreme attention to benign bodily symptoms
     c. help Megan uncover the repressed anxiety causing her symptoms
     d. discourage Megan from seeing her general practitioner

* 7.   All of the following are examples of explicit memory except
     a. how to tie your shoe.
     b. describing the new house you just bought.
     c. telling your best friend about a recent trip to the beach.
     d. describing a toy that you had as a child.

* 8. Recovery from dissociative fugue is
      a. rare.
      b. takes varying amounts of time.
      c. likely only after lengthy therapy.
      d. accomplished in brief therapy.

9. Cognitive scientists studying DID disagree on the role of
    a. explicit memory.
    b. exposure to the media.
    c. therapy.
    d. implicit memory.

10. Goals for the treatment of dissociative identity disorder include
     a. firm limits on socially inappropriate behavior.
     b. maximum personal growth of each alter.
     c. integration of the several personalities.
     d. reliving the trauma that led to the problem.

Short Answer

1. What are the characteristics of hypochondriasis?

2. Distinguish between conversion disorder and somatization disorder.

3. Symptoms of conversion disorder can be difficult to distinguish symptoms of other problems. What are the other problems and why is distinguishing them important?

4. Describe the psychodynamic studies that led to a contemporary revision of Freud's theory of conversions.

5. Describe the importance of genetic and neurobiological factors in somatoform disorders in general.

6. How do behavioral and cognitive therapists approach treatment of somatoform disorders?

7. Describe normal dissociation and give examples.

8.   What is the presumed basis for dissociative disorders in general?

9.   Distinguish between dissociative amnesia and dissociative fugue.

10.   Describe two theories of the etiology of dissociative identity disorder (DID).

Internet Resources

The following are Internet resources to begin exploring the topics in this chapter. Additional general Internet resources are at the end of the introduction chapter.

International Society for the Study of Dissociation has an extensive list of frequently asked questions about dissociation.   www.issd.org

The Skeptic's Dictionary has a free wheeling discussion of views on the existence and nature of dissociative identity disorder.   SkepDic.com/mpd.html

Answers to Self-Test, Chapter 6

Multiple Choice

1. b (p. 162)	2. d (p. 164)	3. d (p. 166)	4. a (p. 167)
5. d (p. 170)	6. c (p. 172)	7. a (p. 177)	8. b (p. 178)
9. d (p. 183-184)	10. c (p. 184)		

Short Answer

1. Preoccupation with fear of having a serious medical illness. (p. 162)

2. Conversion symptoms emphasize a *loss* of functioning while somatization disorder symptoms emphasize *complaints* about loss of functioning. The distinction can be difficult in practice. (p. 162-164)

3. Conversion symptoms are often similar to symptoms of neurological problems. Early studies found that many people diagnosed with conversion disorder actually proved to have medical conditions. (Recent medical advances have improved the situation.) (p. 164-165)

4. Case studies in which individuals with conversions involving blindness would "guess" visual stimuli much better (or worse) than chance. (p. 166)

5. Genetic factors do not appear significant. Body dysmorphic disorder may be similar to obsessive compulsive disorder with similar neurobiological factors. (Neurobiological factors in other somatoform disorders are unclear.) (p. 169)

6. They use a variety of techniques to change a) emotions that trigger concerns b) cognitions about concerns and c) resume healthy activities and decrease reliance on being "sick". (p. 170)

7. Normal dissociation occurs when people become preoccupied and forget things. For example, people may forget where they left their keys, appointments they made, or what they went to the store to get. (p. 174)

8. They are an avoidance response. They protect the individual from remembering traumatic memories that would be painful. (p. 174)

9. Amnesia involves the loss of particular memories (usually about traumatic events). Fugue involves more extensive memory loss. The person loses all memory, including who he/she is, and often leaves home and takes on a new identity. (p. 175-178)

10. One theory is that DID arises from severe childhood abuse. The other is that it is a social role encouraged by overly zealous therapists and/or popular media reports. (p. 182)

7 Stress and Health

Overview

The last two chapters covered psychological disorders linked to anxiety. Traditionally, they were referred to as neuroses. Those in Chapter 5 involved more or less direct difficulties with anxiety. In Chapter 6, the disorders did not directly involve anxiety, but, traditionally, anxiety is believed to underlie them. They were somatoform disorders (involving physical symptoms) and dissociative disorders (involving memory, consciousness, and identity). While many of the problems in Chapter 6 involved physical complaints, they did not involve physically detectable changes in the body. In contrast, the problems covered in Chapter 7 involve physical tissue changes.

It should be clear by now that anxiety is a source of much psychological suffering. Anxiety and stress also have physical effects. Some of these, such as heart disease, ulcers, and asthma, have traditionally been termed psychophysiological disorders. However, that term has been discarded with the realization that stress is a factor in illness and health generally. Chapter 8 discusses stress and health generally, as well as some of the traditional psychophysiological disorders.

After Chapter 7, the text shifts focus. Chapters 8 and 9 cover mood disorders (such as depression) and eating disorders (such as anorexia nervosa). These are more complex problems, at least in terms of research and treatment issues.

Chapter Summary

Psychophysiological disorders are physical diseases produced or influenced in part by psychological factors, including stress, social support, and negative emotions.

Psychophysiological disorders no longer appear as a diagnostic category in the DSM. Instead, the diagnostician can make a diagnosis of psychological factors affecting a medical condition and then note the condition on Axis III. This change reflects the growing realization that life stress is relevant to all diseases and is not limited to those previously considered psychosomatic.

Stress In attempting to understand the complex stress-illness relationship, researchers have focused on precisely defining what stress is; assessing differences in how people cope with perceived stress; and determining how social support impacts the stress-illness relationship.

Theories of the etiology of psychophysiological disorders are diathesis-stress in nature, but differ in whether the diathesis is described in psychological or biological terms. Theories positing a biological diathesis emphasize the effects of allostatic load, or changes in the immune system, that are caused by stress. Theories positing a psychological diathesis focus on such factors as emotional states, personality traits, cognitive appraisals, and specific styles of coping with stress. The most successful accounts of etiology are those that integrate psychological and biological factors.

Cardiovascular Disorders Cardiovascular disorders, which involve the heart and circulatory system, include essential hypertension and coronary heart disease (CHD). While both conditions are complex and multifaceted, their etiologies appear to include a tendency to respond to stress with increases in blood pressure or heart rate. Anger, hostility, cynicism, anxiety, and depression are linked to these conditions.

Asthma Individuals with asthma tend to have respiratory systems that overrespond to allergens or that have been weakened by prior infection. Psychological factors such as anxiety, anger, depression, stressful life events, and family conflict may trigger an asthma attack.

AIDS: A Challenge Acquired immunodeficiency syndrome (AIDS) has psychological elements in that it usually arises from behavior that appears irrational and generally is preventable by psychological means. The primary focus of prevention is to change people's behavior—specifically, to encourage safer sex and to discourage the sharing of needles in intravenous substance abuse.

Treatment Because psychophysiological disorders represent true physical dysfunctions, treatment usually includes medication. The general aim of psychotherapies for these disorders is to reduce stress, anxiety, depression, or anger.

Researchers in the field of behavioral medicine try to find psychological interventions that can improve patients' physiological state by changing unhealthy behaviors and reducing stress. They have developed ways of helping people relax, smoke less, eat fewer fatty foods, and engage in behaviors that can prevent or alleviate illnesses, such as encouraging breast self-examination and adhering to medical treatment recommendations.

Stress management interventions gives people, without diagnosable problems, techniques to cope with the inevitable stress of everyday life. Stress management ameliorates the toll that stress can take on the body.

Learning Goals

1. Be able to distinguish the definitions of stress, coping, and social support

2. Be able to understand the theories of the stress-illness link as well as concept of allostatic load and the basic components of the immune system

3. Be able to describe how psychological factors impact cardiovascular disorders, asthma, and AIDS.

4. Be able to delineate the importance of gender, socioeconomic status, and ethnicity in health.

5. Be able to describe the major psychological treatments for psychophysiological disorders, including psychological approaches to reduce anger, anxiety, and depression, as well as stress management, and biofeedback.

Key Terms

Psychophysiological disorders (p. 189)

Psychological factors affecting medical condition (p. 189)

Behavioral medicine (p. 189)

Health psychology (p. 189)

Coping (p. 191)

Structural social support (p. 193)

Functional social support (p. 193)

Allostatic load (p. 196)

Psychoneuroimmunology (p. 196)

Cytokines (p. 197)

Secretory immunoglobulin A [sIgA] (p. 197)

Interleukin-6 [IL-6] (p. 198)

Anger-in theory (p. 198)

Cardiovascular disorders (p. 200)

Essential hypertension (p. 200)

Type A behavior pattern (p. 202)

Coronary heart disease [CHD] (p. 203)

Angina pectoris (p. 203)

Myocardial infarction (p. 203)

Metabolic syndrome (p. 204)

Asthma (p. 207)

AIDS (acquired immune deficiency syndrome) (p. 211)

Biofeedback (p. 222)

Community psychology (p. 223)

Stress management (p. 225)

Study Questions

1.   Define psychophysiological disorders. How does DSM-IV-TR handle psychophysiological disorders? How does this approach lead to broader understandings of the relationship between stress and health? (p. 189)

What is Stress? (p. 190-194)

2.   Describe three approaches to defining stress and the limitations of each. Describe four dimensions of coping (including positive emotions) and how their effectiveness varies. Summarize studies on the relationship of stress and illness and of coping styles and illness. (p. 190-192)

3.   How do social supports affect health? Describe two types of social support and the ways social supports affect health. Describe a laboratory study showing this relationship. (p. 192-194)

Theories of the Stress-illness Link (p. 194-199)

4.   What kinds of questions are confronted by theories of the stress-illness link? Are these theories compatible with each other? As biological theories, describe allostatic load and the immune system, including two kinds of immunity and two kinds of cells. As psychological theories, describe psychoanalytic and cognitive approaches. (p. 194-199)

Cardiovascular Disorders (p. 200-206)

5.   What is essential hypertension, and how much of a problem is it? Describe the idea and data regarding (a) three ways of studying the relation between psychological stress and blood pressure increases, and (b) three possible diatheses for chronic increases (hypertension). (p. 200-203)

6. Describe two principal forms of coronary heart disease (CHD). What limitation of traditional risk factors for CHD led to a search for diatheses?   What data suggest a role for stress and Type A behavior in CHD? What aspects of Type A behavior appear most important in CHD? What two biological risk factors are involved? (p. 203-206)

Asthma (p. 207-210)

7. What happens in an asthma attack? Regarding the etiology of asthma, what question has been a topic of debate, and what has research found? Summarize research on the role of stressful life events, negative emotions, and the role of the family in asthma. List several biological factors. (p. 207-210)

AIDS: A Challenge for the Behavioral Sciences (p. 211-215)

8. Why is AIDS an appropriate topic for an abnormal psychology textbook? Briefly summarize the scope of the problem, description of the disease, and how it spreads. Describe the success of early and recent AIDS prevention programs. Psychological theory suggests what general approach to AIDS prevention? How successful have such efforts been?   Summarize the success of more intensive programs (at least with men). Give four (or so) reasons why knowledge about AIDS may not be enough. (p. 211-215)

Gender and Health (p. 216-218)

9. Identify mortality and morbidity differences between men and women. Briefly describe four possible reasons for women's decreased mortality. Identify several possible reasons for women's increased morbidity. Finally, describe why excluding women from research studies impacts women's health. (p. 216-218)

Socioeconomic Status, Ethnicity, and Health (p. 218-220)

10. List several possible reasons for the relationship between a) socioeconomic status and health, and b) between ethnicity and health. (p. 218-220)

Treatment of Psychophysiological Disorders (p. 221-225)

11. Why is coordination of medical and psychological interventions needed in treating psychophysiological disorders? Describe more specific programs in five areas: a) hypertension (methods aimed at risk factors, exercise, and, cognitions), b) biofeedback, c) Type A behavior and hostility, d) stress management, and e) cognitive behavioral interventions. (p. 221-225)

Self-Test, Chapter 7
(* Items not covered in Study Questions.)

Multiple Choice

* 1.   A term that was once used for psychophysiological disorders is
      a. somatoform disorders.
      b. somatization disorders.
      c. psychosomatic disorders.
      d. psychomimetic disorders.

2.   Brent copes with the diagnosis of asthma by reading everything he can find about the illness.
     This is an example of
      a. inward-focused coping.
      b. outward-focused coping.
      c. problem-focused coping.
      d. emotion-focused coping.

3.   Celeste is known and liked by everyone on campus. Celeste has high
      a. adaptive social supports.
      b. structural social supports.
      c. functional social supports.
      d. The question cannot be answered without more information.

* 4.   One of the recurrent problems with research on the etiology of psychophysiological disorders is
       that
      a. such studies are difficult to conduct.
      b. research often links stress to self-reports of illness.
      c. research relies too heavily on physician reports of illness rather than patient reports.
      d. psychologists are not knowledgeable about medical illnesses.

5.   An example of a natural immunity would be
      a. cytokines.
      b. allostatic load.
      c. hormones.
      d. sympathetic nervous system.

6.   Mr. O'Brien was told by his physician that his hypertension had no apparent organic cause. This
     is referred to as _____ hypertension.
      a. secondary
      b. dystolic
      c. systolic
      d. essential

7.   Which of the following is <u>not</u> characteristic of the Type A behavior pattern?
      a. cynical
      b. ambitious
      c. unhappy
      d. impatient

8.   The Western Collaborative Group Study provided evidence for the _____ of the Type A construct.
    a. concurrent validity
    b. predictive validity
    c. lack of validity
    d. lack of reliability

9.   Regardless of the original etiology of asthma, most asthma sufferers report
    a. that they can control their attacks.
    b. their attacks are precipitated by anxiety.
    c. attacks appear to come about following physical exertion.
    d. an aura prior to an attack.

10.   All of the following are techniques used in stress management except
    a. arousal reduction.
    b. cognitive restructuring.
    c. biofeedback.
    d. environmental-change approaches.

Short Answer

1.   Why are psychophysiological disorders not a category in DSM-IV-TR?

2.   Why was it difficult to apply Selye's theory of stress to psychology?

3.   Summarize the role of cognitions in stress.

4.   How important is essential hypertension as a health problem?

5.   What do people experience when they have an asthma attack?

6.   Give four or so possible reasons why current AIDS prevention programs are less than effective.

7.   Distinguish between mortality and morbidity.

8.   Give several reasons that low socioeconomic status (SES) is associated with poor health.

9.   Why is coordination of medical and psychological interventions needed in treating psychophysiological disorders?

10.   Describe the treatment for Type A behavior.

Internet Resources

The following are internet resources to begin exploring the topics in this chapter. Additional general internet resources are at the end of the introduction chapter.

American Institute of Stress has information on stress problems and management.   www.stress.org

Stress management and Emotional Wellness Links offers a wide range of links on stress and stress management.   www.imt.net/~randolfi/StressLinks.html

Answers to Self-Test, Chapter 7

Multiple Choice

1. c (p. 189)   2. c (p. 191)   3. b (p. 193)   4. b (p. 195)
5. a (p. 197-198) 6. d (p. 200)   7. c (p. 202)   8. b (p. 205)
9. b (p. 209)   10. c (p. 225)

Short Answer

1. Virtually all physical diseases are recognized as potentially related to psychological factors. (p. 189)

2. It was not clear how to define stressors. People react to life's challenges differently. (p. 190)

3. Stress is related to how people appraise life situations. People who see themselves as unable to cope or have ineffective coping strategies will be stressed more often. (p. 198-199)

4. Called the "silent killer" (because people aren't aware of and don't check their blood pressure), essential hypertension contributes to various cardiovascular disorders, which are the number one killer. (Ten percent of college students have hypertension. Check your blood pressure!) (p. 200)

5. Sudden onset with tightness in chest, wheezing, coughing. Increased fluid in lungs, eyes, etc. Sense of suffocating. (p. 207-208)

6. Current programs provide information on AIDS prevention however people a) are not always rational, b) are not rational during sex, c) may avoid acting on what they know as it's not sexy or suggests lack of trust in their partner, d) may get irritated by repeated advice and urging, or e) may not have access to condoms. (p. 212-213)

7. Mortality refers to death and death rates. Morbidity refers to general healthiness. On average women live longer (lower mortality), but are in poorer general health (lower morbidity). (p. 216)

8. While details are unclear, low SES circumstances encourage people into poor health choices (more liquor stores, fewer exercise opportunities, etc.) They have less access to health care and less insurance. They are exposed to stresses of prejudice and crowded living conditions. (p. 218-220)

9. Medical treatment is needed to relieve immediate symptoms, but psychological treatment to needed to reduce underlying issues. (p. 221)

10. Multifaceted programs encourage more relaxed behaviors (talk slower, listen more), reduce anger and stress from TV and work, change cognitions to stop seeing everything as a challenge that must be met, and reduce negative beliefs and emotions. (p. 224)

8 Mood Disorders

Overview

The previous three chapters covered a wide range of problems related, in one way or another, to anxiety and stress. They included both psychological disorders and the contribution of stress to medical conditions in general.

The text now shifts focus. Chapter 8 discusses mood disorders such as depression and mania. The chapter also discusses suicide, which often, but not always, involves mood disorders. The literature on mood disorders is complex. Physiological and genetic factors have long been studied, both because drugs can be effective in treating them and because individuals with mania experience rapid mood shifts that often seemed otherwise inexplicable. Psychological research has also been extensive, and psychological therapies have proven effective.

After Chapter 8, the text goes on to discuss eating disorders (Chapter 9) and substance-related disorders (Chapter 10). Both seem more related to social and cultural factors. However genetic and physiological diatheses have also been studied.

Chapter Summary

Clinical Descriptions and Epidemiology There are two broad types of mood disorders: depressive disorders and bipolar disorders.

Depressive disorders include major depression and dysthymia, and bipolar disorders include bipolar I disorder, bipolar II disorder, and cyclothymia.

Bipolar I disorder is defined by mania or mixed episodes. Bipolar II disorder is defined by hypomania and episodes of depression. Major depressive disorder, bipolar I disorder, and bipolar II disorder, are episodic. Recurrence is very common in these disorders.

Dysthymia and cyclothymia are characterized by low levels of symptoms that last for at least two years.

Major depression is one of the most common psychiatric disorders, affecting as many as 16.2% of people during their lifetime. Rates of depression are twice as high in women as in men. Bipolar I disorder is much more rare, affecting approximately 1% of people.

Etiology Genetic studies provide evidence that bipolar disorder is strongly heritable and that depression is somewhat heritable.

Neurobiological research has focused on the sensitivity of postsynaptic receptors rather than on the amount of various transmitters, with the strongest evidence for changes in serotonin receptors in depression, and potential changes in the dopamine receptors within the reward system as related to mania.

Bipolar and unipolar disorders seem tied to elevated activity of the amygdala and diminished activity in regions of the prefrontal cortex, the hippocampus, and the anterior cingulate.

Overactivity of the hypothalamic-pituitary-adrenal axis is also found among depressive patients, manifested by high levels of cortisol and poor suppression of cortisol by dexamethasone.

Socioenvironmental models focus on the role of negative life events, lack of social support, and family criticism as triggers for episodes, but also consider ways in which a person with depression may elicit negative responses from others. People with less social skill and those who tend to seek more excessive reassurance are at elevated risk for the development of depression.

Psychological theories of depression include psychoanalytic, emotion and personality, and cognitive models. Psychoanalytic formulations focus on anger turned inward, but this idea has not been supported. Neuroticism appears to consistently predict the onset of depression. Beck's cognitive theory ascribes causal significance to negative schemata and cognitive biases. According to hopelessness theory, low self-esteem or beliefs that an event will have long-term meaningful consequences can instill a sense of hopelessness, which is expressed in a specific set of depressive symptoms called hopelessness depression.

Psychological theories of depression in bipolar disorder are similar to those proposed for unipolar depression. Some researchers have proposed that mania may arise after negative experiences, but others suggest that dysregulation in the reward system in the brain, so that mania can be triggered by life events involving success and unrealistically positive cognitions about future goals.

Treatment Several psychological therapies are effective for depression, including interpersonal therapy, cognitive therapy, social-skills therapy, behavioral activation therapy, and behavioral marital therapy.

The major approaches that have been found to help as adjuncts to medication for bipolar disorder include psychoeducation, family therapy, and cognitive therapy.

Electroconvulsive shock and several antidepressant drugs (tricyclics, selective serotonin reuptake inhibitors, and MAO inhibitors) have proved their worth in lifting depression. Lithium is the best-researched treatment for prevention of mania, but Depakote and Olanzapine also help decrease manic symptoms.

Suicide Men, elderly people, and people who are divorced or widowed are at elevated risk for suicide. Most people who commit suicide meet diagnostic criteria for psychiatric disorders, with more than half experiencing depression. Suicide is at least partially heritable, and neurobiological models focus on serotonin and over-activity in the HPA. Social changes are common precedents to anomic suicide. Individual vulnerability may be tied to difficulty achieving high goals, poor problem-solving, hopelessness, lack of reasons to live, and low life satisfaction.

Several approaches have been taken to prevention. For people with a mental illness, psychological treatments and medications to quell symptoms help reduce suicidality. Many people believe it is important to address suicidality more directly, though. Problem-solving therapy has shown promise in reducing suicidal behavior, but not all results have been positive. Suicide hotlines are found in most cities, but it has been hard to conduct research demonstrating their effectiveness.

Learning Goals

1. Be able to describe the symptoms of depression and mania, the diagnostic criteria for depressive disorders and bipolar disorders, and the epidemiology of these disorders.

2. Be able to discuss the genetic, neurobiological, social, and psychological factors that contribute to the symptoms of mood disorders.

3. Be able to identify the medication and psychological treatments of depressive and manic symptoms and the current views of electroconvulsive therapy.

4. Be able to explain the epidemiology of suicide, the neurobiological, social, and psychological risk factors associated with suicide, and methods for preventing suicide.

To My Students

This chapter covers both depression and the related topic of suicide. Estimates are that 20 percent of students will consider suicide during college. You might consider what you would do if a friend (or you) feels suicidal. You will find some ideas in the chapter. However, you would also want to seek professional help. Most areas of the United States have 24-hour telephone lines for suicide prevention centers as described on pages 267. This would be a good phone number to add to your address book. You can probably get the number from your instructor, college counseling center, or the local mental health clinic. Of course, you can always call "911", but many 911 centers will refer you to another number with people who specialize in suicide help.

Key Terms

Mood disorder (p. 230)

Major depressive disorder [MDD] (p. 231)

Episodic disorder (p. 231)

Dysthymic disorder (p. 231)

Mania (p. 233)

Flight of ideas (p. 233)

Mixed episode (p. 233)

Hypomania (p. 233)

Bipolar I disorder (p. 233)

Bipolar II disorder (p. 234)

Cyclothymic disorder (p. 234)

Seasonal (p. 235)

Rapid cycling (p. 235)

Psychotic features (p. 235)

Catatonic features (p. 235)

Postpartum onset (p. 235)

Melancholic (p. 235)

Norepinephrine (p. 238)

Dopamine (p. 238)

Serotonin (p. 238)

Tryptophan (p. 239)

Second messengers (p. 240)

G-proteins (p. 240)

Amygdala (p. 240)

Hippocampus (p. 240)

Prefrontal cortex (p. 240)

Anterior cingulate (p. 240)

Reward system (p. 242)

HPA axis (p. 242)

Cortisol (p. 242)

Cushing's syndrome (p. 242)

Expressed emotion (p. 244)

Negative affect (p. 246)

Positive affect (p. 246)

Somatic arousal (p. 246)

Neuroticism (p. 246)

Extraversion (p. 246)

Negative triad (p. 247)

Schemata (p. 247)

Cognitive biases (p. 247)

Learned helplessness theory (p. 248)

Attributions (p. 248)

Attributional style (p. 249)

Hopelessness theory (p. 249)

Manic defense (p. 251)

Interpersonal psychotherapy [IPT] (p. 252)

Cognitive therapy (p. 253)

Irrational belief (p. 254)

Behavioral activation therapy [BA] (p. 254)

Mindfulness-based cognitive therapy [MBCT] (p. 254)

Social skills training (p. 254)

Behavioral marital therapy (p. 255)

Psychoeducational approaches (p. 255)

Family-focused treatment [FFT] (p. 255)

Electroconvulsive therapy [ECT [(p. 256)

Monoamine oxidase [MAO] inhibitors (p. 256)

Tricyclic antidepressants (p. 256)

Selective serotonin reuptake inhibitors [SSRIs] (p. 256)

Lithium (p. 259)

Suicide (p. 261)

Egoistic suicide (p. 263)

Altruistic suicide (p. 264)

Anomic suicide (p. 264)

Suicide prevention centers (p. 267)

Study Questions

Clinical Descriptions and Epidemiology of Mood Disorders (p. 230-237)

1. Give at least five different general characteristics of depression (p. 230-231) and mania (p. 233). Distinguish among two depressive disorders (p. 231) and three bipolar disorders (p. 233-234) in DSM-IV-TR. List six subtypes of mood disorders. (p. 235-237)

Etiology of Mood Disorders (p. 237-251)

2. Research has focused on which two mood disorders? How heritable is each? Give two ways in which early neurotransmitter models were not supported and two studies supporting the current model. (p. 237-240)

3.   Identify four brain structures involved in depression and list their functions. What do research studies show, and how might the findings fit together?   Summarize a different kind of study that supports this view. How are the findings for bipolar disorder similar and different?   What does this suggest about the brain's reward system? (p. 240-242)

4.   Regarding the neuroendocrine system in depression, describe the relationship between the amygdala, the HPA axis, and cortisol.   Describe findings from three research areas suggesting cortisol involvement in depression. (p. 242-243)

5.   Describe the role of stressful life events and interpersonal difficulties (three areas of study) in depression, including studies that suggest a causal relationship. How may these factors and neurobiological factors interact in leading to depression? (p. 243-245)

6. According to Freud's theory, what childhood circumstances predispose people to depression? How does loss develop into depression? What is the current status of this theory? Summarize ideas on affect and neuroticism by describing a three-dimensional model of depression and anxiety and the results from three areas of research using the model. (p. 245-247)

7. Describe Beck's cognitive theory of depression in four ideas. Evaluate this theory by describing research on two points. Describe three stages in the evolution of the hopelessness theory of depression. Summarize two studies of this theory. (p. 247-250)

8. Regarding the etiology of bipolar disorder, what events trigger depressive episodes? Describe two models of triggers for manic episodes. (p. 250-251)

Treatment of Mood Disorders (p. 252-260)

9. Regarding psychological treatment of depression, briefly describe interpersonal psychotherapy. Describe cognitive and behavioral components of Beck's cognitive therapy. What is the rationale and method of mindfulness-based cognitive therapy, social-skills training, behavioral activation therapy, and behavioral marital therapy? (p. 252-255)

10. How are medical and psychological treatments used in treating bipolar disorder? What is the general goal of psychological treatment, and why is family-focused treatment often used? (p. 255-256)

11. As biological treatments for mood disorders, describe electroconvulsive therapy, including modern improvements and the advantages and disadvantages of ECT. How common and effective are medications for depression? What are their advantages and disadvantages compared to psychotherapy? (p. 256-257)

12. Describe a NIMH research program on treating depression including, the groups and procedures, five findings, and two controversies   Describe the results of a more recent study designed to answer the controversies. What does it suggest are advantages and disadvantages of cognitive therapy compared to medication? (p. 257-259)

13. What are the advantages and disadvantages of lithium in treating bipolar disorder? What are two reasons it is often given in combination with other medications?   What are the issues in having primary care physicians treat depression? What kind of programs seems to help? (p. 259-260)

Suicide (p. 261-267)

14. Review and be able to recognize 8 points suggested by studies of suicide. As models of suicide, describe the relationship between suicide, depression, and psychological disorders generally.   What do studies suggest about heritability and neurotransmitters in suicide? Socioculturally, what is the impact of media reports of suicide? Summarize Durkheim's sociocultural model of suicide. Identify five psychological models of suicide. (p. 261-266)

15. Identify two general points about preventing suicide and the importance of appropriate help for underlying mental disorders. Summarize Shneidman's approach to suicide treatment and the stance of professional organizations. What are suicide prevention centers, and are they effective? (p. 266-267)

Self-Test, Chapter 8

(* Items not covered in Study Questions.)

Multiple Choice

1. Iris has been feeling depressed most of the time for the past three years. She generally feels inadequate, sleeps a great deal, has trouble concentrating, and avoids social contact. The most likely diagnosis for Iris would be
    a. cyclothymic disorder.
    b. bipolar I disorder.
    c. dysthymic disorder.
    d. hypomania.

* 2. Which of the following is considered to be one of the most severe forms of mental illness?
    a. dysthymic disorder
    b. cyclothymic disorder
    c. hypomania
    d. bipolar I

3. Which of the following statements is true about the heritability of major depressive disorder?
    a. 84% of the variance in whether a person will develop depression is explained by one's environment.
    b. 84% of individuals who have a first-degree relative with major depression will also develop major depression.
    c. 37% of individuals who have a first-degree relative with major depression will also develop major depression.
    d. 37% of the variance in whether a person will develop depression is explained by genes.

4. Researchers can test how sensitive receptors are to fluctuations in serotonin by
    a. measuring the synapses directly.
    b. increasing levels of tryptophan.
    c. depleting levels of tryptophan.
    d. drinking something that contains serotonin agonists.

5. Stella has a history of major depression. Although she is not currently depressed, a researcher puts her in a sad mood by asking her to think about a recent family death. A PET scan of her brain during this mood induction would most likely reveal
    a. that Stella's brain is functioning in the same way as an individual with no depression history.
    b. that Stella's brain has less activity in the part of the brain responsible for planning and executing goals.
    c. that Stella's brain is overactive in the prefrontal cortex.
    d. that Stella is no longer vulnerable to depression.

6. The term expressed emotion is defined as
    a. a person with depression expressing how he/she feels about something.
    b. critical or hostile comments made towards a person with depression.
    c. facial emotions.
    d. negative reactions.

7. Which of the following involves somatic arousal?
    a. anxiety and depression
    b. depression
    c. anxiety
    d. dysthymia

8. Who has the highest risk of suicide?
    a. a gay adolescent male
    b. a twenty-five-year-old stock broker
    c. a fifty-year-old mother of three children
    d. a seventy-year-old grandfather

9. A single man with no friends can no longer bear his loneliness and kills himself. How would this suicide be classified in Durkheim's sociological scheme?
    a. altruistic
    b. egoistic
    c. intrinsic
    d. anomic

10. According to ethical guidelines of professional mental health organizations, if clients make serious suicide threats, the therapist
    a. can break confidentiality to keep the clients from harming themselves.
    b. cannot break confidentiality, but can encourage the clients to voluntarily hospitalize themselves.
    c. must explore the possibility of physician-assisted suicide with the clients.
    d. must either prescribe or refer the clients for the prescription of medication to prevent the clients from harming themselves.

Short Answer

1. List five characteristics of depression (in addition to feeling sad).

2. Describe three research findings that suggest high cortisol levels are involved in depression.

3. Summarize Freud's theory of depression.

4. Describe two research findings supporting Beck's cognitive theory of depression.

5. Summarize the latest version of the hopelessness theory of depression.

6.   Identify one advantage and one disadvantage to drug treatment for serious depression.

7.   Briefly describe interpersonal psychotherapy.

8.   How are medical and psychological treatments often used in treating bipolar disorder?

9.   According to recent NIMH studies, what are the advantages and disadvantages of cognitive therapy versus medication in treating major depression?

10.   Describe Schneidman's approach to suicide prevention.

Internet Resources

The following are internet resources to begin exploring the topics in this chapter. Additional general internet resources are at the end of the introduction chapter.

Bipolar Focus offers information, support and education on Bipolar Disorder.   www.moodswing.org

Child and Adolescent Bipolar Foundation provides a wide range of information including current research and support groups.   www.bpkids.org

Depression and How Psychotherapy and Other Treatments Can Help People Recover has an overview of depression and treatment options.   apa.org/pubinfo/depression.html

Facts about Suicide in Older Adults highlights facts about the high rates of suicide in older adults and includes links to further resources.   www.apa.org/ppo/issues/oldersuicidefact.html

Answers to Self-Test, Chapter 8

Multiple Choice

1. c (p. 231)   2. d (p. 234)   3. d (p. 237)   4. c (p. 239)
5. b (p. 240-242)   6. b (p. 244)   7. c (p. 246)   8. d (p. 262)
9. b (p. 263)   10. a (p. 267)

Short Answer

1. Change (increase or decrease) in sleep, eating, and activity. Loss of interest, concentration, and energy. Social withdrawal. Negative feelings about self, thoughts of suicide. (p. 230)

2. Cushing's syndrome (high cortisol) often produces depressive symptoms. Animals injected with cortisol releasers appear depressed. Drugs that suppress cortisol don't do so in people with depression. (p. 242)

3. People who were over/under gratified in the oral stage become fixated and overly dependent on others. When others die, the person cannot accept (normal) anger at the loss, so the anger turns inward as depression. (In effect "It can't be that she was a bad mother for leaving me so I must be a bad child.") (p. 245-246)

4. People with depression score higher on various scales of negative thinking. More importantly people who score highly are more likely to become depressed after a loss. (p. 247-248)

5. Beliefs that desirable outcomes will not occur and the person is unable to change the situation. They attribute negative experiences to factors, which are internal, stable, and global. Thus, they feel hopeless. (p. 249)

6. Advantage: they hasten recovery at least for some people. Disadvantages: drug side effects, relapse common if drug is discontinued, possible suicide risk. (p. 256-257)

7. Therapist and client select one or two major current interpersonal problems and work to change them by identifying feelings, building skills, etc. (p. 252)

8. In treating bipolar disorder, medication is considered necessary. Psychological treatment is used to educate clients and their families, deal with related problems, and encourage compliance with medication. (p. 255)

9. Both were equally effective. Cognitive therapy was less expensive and more effective in preventing relapse. Medications take effect more quickly, but can have side effects. (p. 259)

10. Schneidman emphasizes helping individuals reduce psychological pain, see options to continued suffering, and pull back from killing themselves. (p. 266)

9 Eating Disorders

Overview

Previous chapters have covered disorders related to anxiety and stress (Chapters 5 through 7) and mood disorders (Chapter 8). Chapter 9 turns to another set of disorders, eating disorders, which more obviously involve social and cultural factors. Eating disorders, such as anorexia nervosa, involve physical changes severe enough to be fatal. Certainly eating disorders involve both anxiety and mood. However, in these disorders, the stress seems to result from cultural pressures on people, especially young women, to focus on their physical appearance.

Chapter 10 discusses another group of disorders that involve obvious social and cultural factors - substance-related disorders. The chapter also covers genetic and physiological diatheses that interact with social pressures.

Chapter 11 covers schizophrenia, which is close to the common terms "crazy" or "psychotic". It is a serious problem, and the research is extensive and complex. Despite these efforts, schizophrenia can only be managed - no "cure" has emerged.

Chapter Summary

Clinical Descriptions The two main eating disorders are anorexia nervosa and bulimia nervosa. Binge eating disorder is being studied for possible inclusion in the DSM-IV. The symptoms of anorexia nervosa include refusal to maintain normal body weight, an intense fear of being fat, a distorted sense of body shape, and, in women, amenorrhea. Anorexia typically begins in the midteens, is ten times more frequent in women than in men, and is comorbid with several other disorders, notably depression. Its course is not favorable, and it can be life threatening. The symptoms of bulimia nervosa include episodes of binge eating followed by purging, fear of being fat, and a distorted body image. Like anorexia, bulimia begins in adolescence, is much more frequent in women than in men, and is comorbid with other diagnoses, such as depression. Prognosis is somewhat more favorable than for anorexia.

Etiology Research in the eating disorders has examined genetics and brain mechanisms. Evidence is consistent with a possible genetic diathesis. Endogenous opioids and serotonin, both of which play a role in mediating hunger and satiety, have been examined in eating disorders. Low levels of both these brain chemicals have been found in such patients, but evidence that these cause eating disorders is limited. Dopamine is also involved with eating, but its role in eating disorders is less well studied.

As sociocultural standards changed to favor a thinner shape as the ideal for women, the frequency of eating disorders increased. The objectification of women's bodies also exerts pressure for women to see themselves through a sociocultural lens. The prevalence of eating disorders is higher in industrialized countries, where the cultural pressure to be thin is strongest. White women tend to have greater body dissatisfaction and general eating disturbances than African American women, though the prevalence rates for actual eating disorders are not markedly different between these two ethnic groups.

On a psychological level, several factors play important roles. Psychodynamic theories of eating disorders emphasize parent–child relationships and personality characteristics. Research on characteristics of families with an eating-disordered child have yielded different data depending on how the data were collected. Reports of patients show high levels of conflict, but actual observations of the families do not find them especially deviant. Studies of personality have found that patients with eating disorders are high in neuroticism and perfectionism and low in self-esteem. Many women with eating disorders report being abused as children, but early abuse does not appear to be a specific risk factor for eating disorders.

Cognitive behavioral theories of eating disorders propose that fear of being fat and body-image distortion make weight loss a powerful reinforcer. Among patients with bulimia nervosa, negative affect and stress precipitate binges that create anxiety, which is then relieved by purging.

Treatment   The main neurobiological treatment of eating disorders is the use of antidepressants. Although somewhat effective, drop-out rates from drug-treatment programs are high and relapse is common when patients stop taking the medication. Treatment of anorexia often requires hospitalization to reduce the medical complications of the disorder. Providing reinforcers for weight gain, such as visits from friends, has been somewhat successful, but no treatment has yet been shown to produce long-term maintenance of weight gain.

Cognitive behavioral treatment for bulimia focuses on questioning society's standards for physical attractiveness, challenging beliefs that encourage severe food restriction, and developing normal eating patterns. Outcomes are promising, both in the short and long term.

Learning Goals

1.   Be able to distinguish the symptoms associated with anorexia, bulimia, and binge eating disorder and to be able to distinguish among the different eating disorders.

2.   Be able to describe the neurobiological, sociocultural, and psychological factors implicated in the etiology of eating disorders.

3.   Be able to discuss the issues surrounding the growing epidemic of obesity in the United States.

4.   Be able to describe the methods of treatment for eating disorders and the evidence supporting their effectiveness.

Key Terms

Anorexia nervosa (p. 271)

Bulimia nervosa (p. 273)

Body mass index [BMI] (p. 275)

Binge eating disorder (p. 275)

Obese (p. 276)

Study Questions

Clinical Descriptions of Eating Disorders (p. 271-276)

1.   Three diagnostic labels are described. For each label, summarize the (a) distinguishing features, (b) subtypes, (c) physical changes, and (d) prognosis. (Note that binge eating disorder is a tentative label and not yet well understood.) (p. 271-276)

Etiology of Eating Disorders (p. 278-290)

2.   Under biological factors, what data suggest a genetic contribution to eating disorders? Identify four possible neurobiological factors and the current status of research on each. Identify two general cautions regarding this research. (p. 278-280)

3.   Briefly describe sociocultural factors in eating disorders in four areas: changing cultural standards, gender influences, cross-cultural studies, and ethnic differences. (p. 280-284)

4.   Summarize two psychodynamic views on eating disorders. Explain the need to be cautious in studying personality and eating disorders. Identify several personality variables characteristic of anorexia and bulimia.   Summarize research on families and eating disorders and the rationale of Minuchin's theory. Summarize research on child abuse and eating disorders. (p. 284-288)

5.   Summarize cognitive-behavioral views on anorexia nervosa and bulimia nervosa. What factors are confirmed in the "tasting" research of Polivy and others? (p. 288-289)

TREATMENT OF EATING DISORDERS (P. 290-294)

6.   Summarize the effectiveness of medication in the treatment of bulimia and of anorexia. In the case of bulimia, include two problems of medications. (p. 290-291)

7.   Psychological treatment of anorexia involves two tiers. Describe the goals, methods, and effectiveness of each. As part of the second tier include Minuchin's family therapy approach. (p. 291-292)

8.   Describe a cognitive-behavioral approach to the treatment of bulimia. Include description of both behavioral methods (to alter actual eating) and cognitive methods (to alter beliefs). (p. 292-293)

9.   Describe the outcomes of cognitive-behavioral treatments for bulimia including: effects on other problems, comparisons with biological and interpersonal therapies, and remaining problems. (p. 293-294)

10.   Describe three possible approaches to preventing eating disorders.   Describe a recent study comparing these approaches and implications for future prevention efforts. (p. 294)

Self-Test, Chapter 9

(* Items not covered in Study Questions.)

Multiple Choice

1. Weight loss in anorexia nervosa is achieved through
    a. dieting.
    b. self-induced vomiting.
    c. excessive exercise.
    d. all of the above are ways in which people with anorexia lose weight.

2. What diagnosis is most appropriate for Kristi? Her weight is stable, but she reports that, several times a week, she "loses control" and "stuffs her face" eating lots of cookies and ice cream, then throws up by tickling her throat.
    a. anorexia nervosa
    b. bulimia nervosa
    c. binge eating disorder
    d. she would not be diagnosed because her weight is stable

3. Nonpurging bulimics, as opposed to purging types, can
    a. be severely underweight.
    b. engage in excessive exercise.
    c. make themselves vomit.
    d. none of the above; there is no nonpurging type of bulimia.

4. Which brain structure has been hypothesized to play a role in eating disorders?
    a. frontal lobe
    b. hippocampus
    c. hypothalamus
    d. pituitary gland

5. The incidence of eating disorders has been rising steadily since the 1950s. This provides the best evidence for the _____ theory of eating disorder.
    a. biological
    b. sociocultural
    c. psychodynamic
    d. family systems

6. Cultural influences on eating disorders are suggested by the fact that eating disorders are more common
    a. when less emphasis in placed on being thin.
    b. among low socioeconomic groups.
    c. among women who are overweight.
    d. in industrialized societies.

7. Which of the following has been proposed as part of the psychodynamic view of eating disorders?
    a. disturbed parent-child relationships
    b. not growing up sexually
    c. low-self esteem
    d. all of the above

8. Positive reinforcement for dieting is sometimes derived from
    a. a sense of mastery and control associated with dieting.
    b. reductions in hunger as one loses more weight.
    c. attention from others as more weight is lost.
    d. decreased negative body image associated with lower weight.

9. Which of the following is not part of cognitive-behavioral treatment of bulimia?
    a. identification of binge-triggering foods to be avoided
    b. encouragement to question society's standards of attractiveness
    c. encouragement to eat regular meals and snacks
    d. relaxation to control urges to vomit

10. Which of the following is a remaining problem in the cognitive-behavioral treatment of bulimia?
    a. treatment is lengthy and expensive
    b. the effective components have not been studied
    c. overall success rates are too low
    d. treatment is not effective with males

Short Answer

1. What data lead us to believe there a genetic diathesis for eating disorders?

2. What has research shown about the families of individuals with eating disorders?

3. What is the relationship between child abuse and eating disorders?

4. Describe what Polivy and others did in their "tasting" research studies.

5. Summarize the effectiveness of medication treatments for eating disorders.

6. Describe the psychological treatment of anorexia nervosa.

7. Describe what happens in Minuchin's family lunch technique for treating anorexia.

8.   Describe cognitive methods to alter the beliefs of bulimic individuals.

9.   How effective are cognitive-behavioral treatments for bulimia? Explain briefly.

10.   According to recent research what approaches may be most effective in preventing eating disorders?

Internet Resources

The following are internet resources to begin exploring the topics in this chapter. Additional general internet resources are at the end of the introduction chapter.

National Eating Disorders Association offers information on all eating disorders and links to other related websites.   www.nationaleatingdisorders.org

The Something Fishy Website on Eating Disorders is a recovery-oriented website with many links and information.   www.something-fishy.org

Answers to Self-Test, Chapter 9

Multiple Choice

1. d (p. 271)   2. b (p. 273-274)   3. b (p. 274)   4. c (p. 279)
5. b (p. 280-281)   6. d (p. 283)   7. d (p. 284)   8. a (p. 288)
9. a (p. 292)   10. c (p. 293-294)

Short Answer

1. Eating disorders are much more likely among close relatives. Higher concordance in MZ than DZ twins. Linkage analysis results. These suggest a genetic diathesis, although adoptee studies have not been done. (p. 278)

2. Variable results. Disturbed relations and low parental support are suggested, but may be a result of eating disorder or of problems in general. Direct observational studies suggest few differences. (p. 286-287)

3. Reported child abuse is higher in individuals with eating disorders and many other problems so it may not be specific to eating disorders. It may be necessary to focus on details of the abuse. (p. 287-288)

4. Participants drink a high-calorie milk shake (a "preload") then rate ice creams. Afterward, they may eat the ice cream. People high in restrained dieting eat more ice cream. (p. 289)

5. Anti-depressants are effective in treating individuals with bulimia, although many drop out, and the effects last only as long as the drug is taken. Drugs have not been effective in anorexia. (p. 290-291)

6. First stage is weight gain by reinforcing eating and may require hospitalization. Second stage is to maintain weight gain often by working with the family. (p. 291)

7. Therapist asks parents (one at a time) to get the child to eat. They are expected to fail, but now they cannot blame each other and are helped to unite in the effort. (p. 291-292)

8. Urged to identify, question, and change beliefs that weight is vital to acceptance by self and others and that only extreme dieting can control weight. (p. 292)

9. They are promising. They are more effective than medication and equal or superior to IPT. However, they are effective only about half the time. (p. 292-294)

10. Research comparing different methods suggests methods should be interactive, include adolescents age 15 or older, include all females, and have multiple sessions. (p. 291)

10 Substance-Related Disorders

Overview

The previous chapter covered eating disorders in which social and cultural factors appeared important. Social and cultural factors are also important in substance related disorders, the subject of this chapter. However genetics and physiology continue to be considered as predisposing factors.

The next chapter, Chapter 11, covers schizophrenia or, loosely, psychosis. Schizophrenia has been widely studied, and the research is complex. Despite much effort, the best we can do is manage schizophrenia. It remains a serious personal and social problem.

Chapters 12 and 13 cover more overtly social problems. Chapter 12 covers personality disorders in which persistent and maladaptive personality traits or behaviors cause difficulty for the individual and others. The most well known personality disorder is antisocial personality disorder (or psychopath) characterized by antisocial behavior and/or by lack of guilt over such behavior. Chapter 13 discusses a wide range of disorders involving sexual behavior.

Many of these problems involve behaviors that are maladaptive or socially unacceptable, but not necessarily "disordered" in the traditional sense. Many are more bothersome to others than to the person involved. At times, it can be difficult to decide if they are psychological, legal, or moral/ethical problems. As a result, they can present dilemmas for treatment personnel.

The text's coverage of specific problems will conclude with Chapters 14 and 15, which deal with issues and disorders of childhood and old age.

Chapter Summary

Clinical Descriptions Using substances to alter mood and consciousness is a common human characteristic, and so, too, is the tendency to abuse them. DSM-IV-TR distinguishes between substance dependence and substance abuse. Dependence refers to a compulsive pattern of substance use and consequent serious psychological and physical impairments, often including tolerance and withdrawal. Substance abuse is a less serious problem in which drug use leads to failure to meet obligations and to interpersonal and legal problems.

Alcohol has a variety of short-term and long-term effects on human beings, ranging from poor judgment and impaired motor coordination to chronic health problems.

People can become dependent on nicotine, most often via smoking cigarettes. Despite somberly phrased warnings from public-health officials, it continues to be used. Medical problems associated with long-term cigarette smoking include many cancers, emphysema, and cardiovascular disease. Moreover, the health hazards of smoking are not restricted to those who smoke; secondhand (or environmental) smoke can also cause lung damage and other problems.

Recent trends indicate that marijuana use declined in the 1980s, increased in the 1990s, and has leveled off since then. When used regularly, marijuana can damage the lungs and cardiovascular system and lead to cognitive impairments. Constituents of marijuana may also adversely affect heart function in people who already have coronary problems, and pulmonary function. Further, tolerance to marijuana can develop. Ironically, just as the possible dangers of marijuana began to be uncovered, it was found to have therapeutic effects, easing the nausea of cancer patients undergoing chemotherapy and the discomfort associated with AIDS.

Opiates slow the activities of the body and, in moderate doses, are used to relieve pain and induce sleep. Heroin has been a focus of concern because usage is up and stronger varieties have become available. Another group is the synthetic sedatives and tranquilizers. Barbiturates have been implicated in both intentional and accidental suicides; they are particularly lethal when taken with alcohol.

Stimulants, which include amphetamines and cocaine, act on the brain and the sympathetic nervous system to increase alertness and motor activity. Tolerance and withdrawal are associated with all these drugs. Methamphetamine abuse, a derivative of amphetamine, has risen dramatically since the 1990s.

The hallucinogens—LSD, mescaline, and psilocybin—alter or expand consciousness. Their use reflects humankind's desire not only to escape from unpleasant realities, but also to explore inner space. Use of the hallucinogen-like drug, Ecstasy, has dramatically risen, and it is also considered a threat to health. PCP use often leads to violence.

Etiology Several factors are related to the etiology of substance abuse and dependence. Sociocultural variables, such as attitudes toward the substance, peer pressure, and how the substance is portrayed by the media, are all related to how frequently a substance is used. Many substances are used to alter mood (for example, to reduce tension or increase positive affect), and people with certain personality traits, such as those high in negative affect or psychopathy, are especially likely to use drugs. Cognitive variables, such as the expectation that the drug will yield positive effects, are also important. Finally, neurobiological factors, most notably a genetic predisposition or diathesis and the brain's reward pathways, appear to play a role in the use of some substances.

Treatment Treatments of all kinds have been used to help people refrain from the use of both legal drugs (e.g., alcohol and nicotine) and illegal drugs (e.g., heroin and cocaine). Biological treatments have attempted to release users from their dependency often by substituting another drug. Some benefits have been observed for treatments using such drugs as clonidine, naltrexone, and methadone. Nicotine replacement via gum, patches, or inhalers has met with some success in reducing cigarette smoking. None of these approaches appears to lead to enduring change, however, unless accompanied by psychological treatments with such goals as helping patients resist pressures to indulge, cope with normal life stress, control emotions without relying on chemicals, and make use of social supports, such as Alcoholics Anonymous.

Since it is far easier never to begin using drugs than to stop using them, considerable effort has been expended in recent years to prevent substance abuse by implementing educational and social programs to equip young people to develop their lives without a reliance on drugs.

Learning Goals

1. Be able to differentiate between substance dependence and abuse

2. Be able to describe the epidemiology and symptoms of drug and alcohol abuse and dependence

3. Be able to understand the major etiological factors for substance-related disorders, including sociocultural factors, mood and expectancy effects, genetic factors, and neurobiological factors.

4. Be able to describe the approaches to treating substance related disorders, including psychological treatments, medications, and drug substitution treatments.

5. Be able to delineate the major approaches to prevention of substance-related disorders.

Key Terms

Substance-related disorders (p. 296)

Substance dependence (p. 297)

Addiction (p. 297)

Tolerance (p. 297)

Withdrawal (p. 297)

Substance abuse (p. 297)

Delirium tremens (DTs) (p. 298)

Polydrug abuse (p. 299)

Fetal alcohol syndrome [FAS] (p. 302)

Nicotine (p. 303)

Secondhand smoke (p. 305)

Marijuana (p. 306)

Hashish (p. 306)

Opiates (p. 310)

Opium (p. 310)

Morphine (p. 310)

Heroin (p. 311)

Hydrocodone (p. 311)

Oxycodone (p. 311)

Barbiturates (p. 312)

Stimulants (p. 313)

Amphetamines (p. 313)

Caffeine (p. 314)

Methamphetamine (p. 315)

Cocaine (p. 316)

Crack (p. 317)

LSD (p. 317)

Hallucinogen (p. 317)

Flashback (p. 318)

Mescaline (p. 318)

Psilocybin (p. 318)

Ecstasy (p. 319)

MDMA (p. 319)

MDA (p. 319)

PCP (p. 320)

Nitrous oxide (p. 321)

Detoxification (p. 331)

Aversion therapy (p. 334)

Controlled drinking (p. 334)

Antabuse (p. 335)

Methadone (p. 342)

Cross-dependent (p. 342)

Study Questions

Clinical Descriptions, Prevalence, and Effects of Substance-Related Disorders (p. 296-320)

1.   Identify and distinguish between substance dependence and substance abuse in DSM-IV-TR. What are the indicators of alcohol dependence and of alcohol abuse? (p. 298)   Summarize the prevalence and patterns of alcohol abuse, especially among college students.   Summarize current thinking on the course of the disorder. Describe the short-term and long-term effects of alcohol abuse in about three points each. (p. 297-303)

2.   Summarize the prevalence and major health consequences of smoking.   What are the consequences of secondhand smoke? (p. 303-305)

3.   Describe changes in the prevalence of marijuana use. Summarize the short-term and long-term psychological and bodily effects. What are the therapeutic effects of marijuana? (p. 306-309)

4.   The text identifies two groups of sedatives and two groups of stimulants. For each group, describe the a) major drugs, b) short-term psychological and physical effects, c) tolerance and withdrawal effects, and d) social consequences. (p. 310-317)

5.   What are the general effects of hallucinogens, and what variables influence their effects? What are two potential dangers? What is known about the short-term and long-term effects of ecstasy and PCP? (p. 318-320)

Etiology of Substance-Related Disorders (p. 321-330)

6.   Explain the idea that the etiology of substance-related disorders is a developmental process. Identify five sociocultural variables affecting abuse and dependence (starting with cross-national variations). (p. 321-325)

7.   The text describes five psychological variables in substance abuse. For mood alteration, describe the relationship between tension-reduction and a) distraction, b) consumption and stress, and c) mood. Describe the role of expectancies, beliefs, other psychopathologies, and cues and cravings. (p. 325-328)

8.   Describe genetic diatheses for alcoholism and smoking. Describe a neurobiological factor and the incentive-sensitization theory. (p. 328-330)

Treatment of Substance-Related Disorders (p. 331-344)

9.   Identify eight approaches or components to psychological treatment of alcohol abuse and dependence. For each, describe what it does and its effectiveness. (p. 331-337)

10.   The book identifies six psychological and three medication approaches to the treatment of smoking. Describe each and its effectiveness (if known). (p. 338-340)

11.   What is the central or first step in treating drug addiction? Describe and evaluate five examples of psychological approaches to the treatment of drug abuse. For medical approaches describe two widely used programs for heroin dependence, two recent efforts to address cocaine dependence, and one effort to address methamphetamine dependence. (p. 340-344)

Prevention of Substance-Related Disorders (p. 344-348)

12.   Why is prevention of substance-related disorders important? In preventing drug abuse, how effective are school-based programs?   In preventing smoking, identify two promising approaches and six common components of school-based programs. Why is relapse prevention important? What is the general approach for alcoholism? Describe a cognitive approach for former smokers. (p. 344-347)

Self-Test, Chapter 10

(* Items not covered in Study Questions.)

Multiple Choice

* 1. Wanda drinks almost a quart of gin a day, may remain intoxicated for two or three consecutive days, and takes Valium every night to calm her nerves and get to sleep. Her problem is referred to as
    a. polydrug abuse.
    b. synergistic abuse.
    c. additive drug abuse.
    d. substance intoxication.

2. Fetal alcohol syndrome refers to
    a. alcohol addiction in infants whose mothers drank during pregnancy.
    b. the theory that alcoholism is transmitted genetically.
    c. mental retardation in infants whose mothers drank during pregnancy.
    d. the tendency of alcoholics to regress to very early stages of development.

* 3. Which group is at lowest risk for lung cancer due to smoking?
    a. Native Americans
    b. Afro-Americans
    c. Asian-Americans
    d. Hispanic-Americans

4. What recent trend has been observed in the prevalence of marijuana use?
    a. steady decline since the 1970s
    b. dramatic increase since decriminalization
    c. an increase in the 1990s which has remained steady since then
    d. dramatic decrease, likely due to the "war on drugs" and program such as "DARE"

5. One major caution in taking marijuana for therapeutic reasons is
    a. the highly addictive features of the drug.
    b. the rate at which one develops tolerance for the drug.
    c. decreased immune functioning.
    d. difficulties associated with withdrawal.

6. Withdrawal from which drug is most likely to be fatal?
    a. cocaine
    b. LSD
    c. barbiturates
    d. marijuana

* 7. Mescaline is a form of
    a. marijuana.
    b. cocaine.
    c. hallucinogen.
    d. ecstacy.

8. Why was the manufacturer of Camel cigarettes asked to stop running ads featuring "Joe Camel"?
    a. They were considered false advertising because of their claims that smoking in moderation is not harmful to health.
    b. They were felt to be aimed at encouraging minors to smoke.
    c. They were found to violate free speech laws.
    d. They were felt to be leading to higher smoking rates among older adults, who are most prone to develop smoking-related health problems.

9. Recent research suggests that a problem with Alcoholics Anonymous is
    a. the lack of professional involvement.
    b. that it is no better than the passage of time.
    c. sometimes people learn other ways to drink by hearing stories from other members.
    d. many people drop out, and success rates do not effectively account for these people.

10. Recent research on treatment for methamphetamine dependence
    a. indicated that Matrix and treatment-as-usual appeared to be equally effective in reducing methamphetamine use after 6 months.
    b. indicated that Matrix is much more effective than treatment-as-usual.
    c. utilizes methadone.
    d. suggests that antabuse may be helpful.

Short Answer

1. How serious is secondhand smoke? Explain.

2. What are the long-term psychological and physical effects of marijuana abuse?

3. List three groups of stimulant drugs discussed in the text (other than caffeine).

4. Describe two dangers of taking hallucinogens such as LSD.

5. Describe the role of beliefs as a psychological variable in substance abuse.

6. What appears to be inherited as a genetic predisposition to alcoholism?

7. How does disulfiram or antabuse discourage alcoholics from drinking?

8.   Identify three medication approaches to the treatment of nicotine addiction.

9.   What happens in self-help programs for drug addiction?

10.   What is the rationale of substance abuse prevention programs?

Internet Resources

The following are internet resources to begin exploring the topics in this chapter. Additional general internet resources are at the end of the introduction chapter.

Alcoholics Anonymous has a wealth of information on AA, including links to local AA groups.

www.alcoholics-anonymous.org

Cocaine Anonymous offers 12-step programs for users of cocaine and related drugs.   www.ca.org

National clearinghouse for Alcohol and Drug information is the US Department of Health and Human Services' website with a wide range of information, resources, and publications on virtually all drugs.   www.health.org

Web of addictions has links to information, groups, meetings, and help on a wide range of addictions.   www.well.com/user/woa

Answers to Self-Test, Chapter 10

Multiple Choice

1. a (p. 299)   2. c (p. 302)   3. c (p. 305)   4. c (p. 306)
5. c (p. 309)   6. c (p. 313)   7. c (p. 318)   8. b (p. 324)
9. d (p. 333)   10. a (p. 344)

Short Answer

1.   Quite serious. Kills 40,000 per year. Second-hand smoke contains higher concentrations than inhaled smoke of some toxins. Problems include lung damage, cardiovascular disease, birth complications, and respiratory infections. (p. 305)

2.   Research is unclear. Psychological effects may include slight loss of learning and memory. Physical effects are surely similar to nicotine. Addiction is unclear, but possible with heavy use. (p. 306-308)

3.   Stimulants include cocaine, amphetamines, and methamphetamine. (p. 313-316)

4.   Dangers include acute anxiety or panic attacks (a "bad trip") and flashbacks afterward. (p. 318)

5.   Abuse is associated with individual beliefs about the risks of using the substance and the prevalence with which others are abusing it. (p. 327)

6.   The ability to tolerate and drink large quantities of alcohol. (p. 328-329)

7.   Producing violent vomiting if one drinks alcohol after taking it. (p. 335)

8.   Three approaches are nicotine gum, nicotine patches, and anti-depressants (as some people who quit experience temporary depression). (p. 339-340)

9.   Residential programs remove addicts from social pressures, support nonuse, provide charismatic role models, include confrontive group therapy, and respect addicts as human beings. (p. 341-342)

10.   Prevention, especially with adolescents, is much easier and more effective than treatment after the problem develops. (p. 344-346)

11 Schizophrenia

Overview

Chapters 9 and 10 discussed two disorders that involved a wide range of genetic, physiological, and psychological/social factors. Schizophrenia (Chapter 11) has led to even more extensive study, at least in part because no overt cure exists for this serious disorder.

Of all the disorders covered in the text, schizophrenia comes closest to the common understanding of being "crazy". Despite extensive study, it remains a major concern both socially and scientifically. Despite recent advances, no cure for schizophrenia has emerged. Currently, a combination of approaches emphasizing drugs can manage, but not cure, schizophrenia. People with schizophrenia remain a major portion of mental hospital and health clinic patients.

After Chapter 11, the focus of the text shifts to disorders that often seem to be more social and behavioral in nature. These include personality disorders such as antisocial personality disorder (Chapter 12), and sexual and gender identity disorders (Chapter 13). These problems do not easily fit traditional views of what constitutes a psychological disorder. Many involve behaviors that are more problematic for others than the individual. In some cases the individual does not appear disturbed in any obvious way aside from the problematic behavior itself. Such problems raise new questions for psychology and society.

Chapter Summary

Clinical Description The symptoms of schizophrenia involve disturbances in several major areas, including thought, perception and attention, motor behavior, affect, and life functioning. Symptoms are typically divided into positive, negative, and disorganized categories. Positive symptoms include excesses and distortions, such as delusions and hallucinations. Negative symptoms are behavioral deficits, such as flat affect, avolition, alogia, and anhedonia. Disorganized symptoms include disorganized speech and behavior. Other symptoms include catatonia and inappropriate affect.

The DSM-IV-TR includes several subtypes of schizophrenia, including disorganized, catatonic, and paranoid. These subtypes are based on the prominence of particular symptoms (e.g., delusions in the paranoid subtype) and reflect the variations in behavior found among people diagnosed with schizophrenia. However, there is considerable overlap among the subtypes, and they have little predictive validity.

Etiology The evidence for genetic transmission of schizophrenia is impressive. Family and twin studies suggest a genetic component. Adoption studies show a strong relationship between having a schizophrenic parent and the likelihood of developing the disorder, typically in early adulthood. Molecular genetics studies are still in need of replication. The most promising findings to date seem to indicate genes such as DTNBP1, NGR1, and COMT are involved.

The genetic predisposition to develop schizophrenia may involve neurotransmitters. It appears that increased sensitivity of dopamine receptors in the limbic area of the brain is related to the positive symptoms of schizophrenia. The negative symptoms may be due to dopamine underactivity in the prefrontal cortex. Other neurotransmitters, such as serotonin, glutamate, and GABA, may also be involved.

The brains of some patients with schizophrenia have enlarged ventricles and problems with the prefrontal cortex. Some of these structural abnormalities could result from maternal viral infection during the second trimester of pregnancy or from damage sustained during a difficult birth.

The diagnosis of schizophrenia is most frequently applied to people of the lowest socioeconomic status, apparently because of downward social mobility created by the disorder. In addition, vague communications and conflicts are evident in the family life of patients with schizophrenia, though it is less clear if these contribute to their disorder. High levels of expressed emotion in families, as well as increases in general life stress, have been shown to be an important determinant of relapse. Developmental studies have identified problems in childhood that were there prior to the onset of schizophrenia, but these studies were not designed to predict schizophrenia, so it is difficult to interpret the findings. High-risk studies suggest that the causes of positive and negative symptoms may be different. Other studies have found cognitive problems in childhood to predict the onset of adult psychopathology, but not specifically schizophrenia.

Treatment   Antipsychotic drugs, especially the phenothiazines, have been widely used to treat schizophrenia since the 1950s. Atypical antipsychotic drugs, such as clozapine and risperidone are also effective and produce fewer motor side effects, though they have their own set of side effects. Drugs alone are not a completely effective treatment though, as patients with schizophrenia need to be taught or retaught ways of dealing with the challenges of everyday life.

The efficacy of psychoanalytic treatments has not been supported by evidence. In contrast, family therapy aimed at reducing high levels of expressed emotion has been shown to be valuable in preventing relapse. In addition, social-skills training and various cognitive behavioral therapies have helped patients meet the inevitable stresses of family and community living and lead more ordered and constructive lives within an institution. Recent efforts to change the thinking of people with schizophrenia are showing promise as well.

The most promising approaches to treatment today emphasize the importance of both pharmacological and psychosocial interventions. Unfortunately, such integrated treatments are not widely available.

Learning Goals

1. Be able to describe the clinical symptoms of schizophrenia, including positive, negative, and disorganized symptoms.

2. Be able to differentiate the genetic factors, both behavioral and molecular, in the etiology of schizophrenia.

3. Be able to discuss how the brain has been implicated in schizophrenia, both in studies of etiology and in treatment

4. Be able to describe the role of stress and other psychosocial factors in the etiology and relapse of schizophrenia.

5. Be able to distinguish between the medication treatments and psychological treatments for schizophrenia.

> **To My Students**
>
> Schizophrenia is a serious and complex problem. Traditional paradigms have generated a tremendous amount of research. Unfortunately, no paradigm has proven highly useful, and our understanding of this problem remains limited.
>
> As a result, this chapter spends little time describing paradigms and considerable time summarizing research. At times the discussion becomes unavoidably complex, especially when summarizing the genetic and physiological research. You may want to refer to the basic discussion of these topics in Chapter 2 of the text.
>
> The study questions indicate the core ideas to look for as you study. Take your time and ask your instructor if you have questions.

Key Terms

Schizophrenia (p. 350)

Positive symptoms (p. 351)

Delusions (p. 351)

Hallucinations (p. 352)

Negative symptoms (p. 353)

Avolition (p. 353)

Alogia (p. 353)

Anhedonia (p. 354)

Flat affect (p. 354)

Asociality (p. 354)

Disorganized symptoms (p. 354)

Disorganized speech (p. 354)

Loose associations (p. 355)

Disorganized behavior (p. 355)

Catatonia (p. 356)

Catatonic immobility (p. 356)

Inappropriate affect (p. 356)

Disorganized schizophrenia (p. 356)

Catatonic schizophrenia (p. 356)

Dementia praecox (p. 357)

Paranoid schizophrenia (p. 358)

Grandiose delusions (p. 358)

Ideas of reference (p. 358)

Undifferentiated schizophrenia (p. 358)

Residual schizophrenia (p. 358)

Schizophreniform disorder (p. 358)

Brief psychotic disorder (p. 358)

Schizoaffective disorder (p. 358)

Delusional disorder (p. 358)

Prefrontal cortex (p. 362)

Dopamine theory (p. 363)

Sociogenic hypothesis (p. 368)

Social-selection theory (p. 368-369)

Expressed emotion [EE] (p. 370)

Antipsychotic drugs (p. 373)

Atypical antipsychotic drugs (p. 376)

Social-skills training (p. 378)

Cognitive enhancement therapy [CET] (p. 381)

Personal therapy (p. 381)

Study Questions

Clinical Descriptions of Schizophrenia (p. 350-359)

1. How serious a problem is schizophrenia (in the middle of p. 350)? Summarize eleven symptoms of schizophrenia organized into four categories. Give examples of the various symptoms explaining why they fit into the various categories. (p. 350-356)

2.   Give several distinguishing characteristics of each of the three subtypes of schizophrenia in DSM-IV-TR. Identify three limitations of these subtypes. (p. 356-358)

Etiology of Schizophrenia (p. 359-372)

3.   Describe the results and limitations of three behavior genetics approaches to studying schizophrenia.   Three molecular genetics approaches are identified: linkage analysis, association studies and, association studies with cognitive functions.   Describe these approaches and current results.   Evaluate the genetic research in terms of a) genetic roles in causing schizophrenia, b) limitations, and c) strength of the research. (p. 359-363)

4.   Discuss the development of the dopamine theory by explaining the following. What two facts originally led to interest in dopamine? As studies progressed, what finding did not support the theory, and how was the theory revised?   What suggested dopamine is related to positive symptoms? (p. 363-364)

5. In the subsequent dopamine theory, how could different neural pathways allow prefrontal underactivity to affect both negative symptoms and, indirectly, positive symptoms? Identify two weaknesses of current dopamine theory and the response of researchers. What two other neurotransmitters are being studied? (p. 364-365)

6. Summarize research results implicating two brain structures in schizophrenia. Describe two findings suggesting these differences may result from congenital and developmental factors. (p. 365-367)

7. If neurological theories are correct, what does this suggest about psychological factors in schizophrenia? What is the relationship between social class and schizophrenia? (What does it mean to say there is a "sharp upturn"?) Describe two theories of this relationship and two studies comparing the theories. What does the text conclude? (p. 368-369)

8.   Evaluate the role of the family in schizophrenia by describing a) an early (and discredited) theory, b) general results and limitations of studies of family influence, and c) family effects on relapse including data suggesting bidirectionality.   In studying developmental factors, how are most studies limited, and how do high-risk studies help?   What have high-risk studies found regarding a) positive and negative symptoms, and b) cortical grey matter? (p. 369-372)

Treatment of Schizophrenia (p. 372-384)

9.   What are the benefits of and the problems with traditional antipsychotic drugs and newer atypical antipsychotics?   What are the psychological benefits of atypical antipsychotics? Describe their use among ethnic minorities. Describe current work toward developing new drugs and the overall importance of drug treatments. (p. 373-377)

10.   The text describes eight psychological treatment approaches. For each, describe the a) rationale, b) method, and c) effectiveness. Describe remaining challenges in terms of providing optimal treatment and dealing with drug abuse. (p. 378-384)

Self-Test, Chapter 11

(* Items not covered in Study Questions.)

Multiple Choice

* 1. Which of the following is required in order to make a diagnosis of schizophrenia?
      a. hallucinations
      b. disorganized speech
      c. delusions
      d. none of the above

2. Joanna, a 30-year-old woman with schizophrenia, believes that everyone can hear her thoughts. She hides in her room for fear that the men she encounters will hear her thoughts about becoming intimate with them. This is an example of
      a. hallucination.
      b. alogia.
      c. delusion.
      d. derailment.

3. Formal thought disorder in schizophrenia refers to
      a. delusions.
      b. anhedonia.
      c. disorganized speech.
      d. hallucinations.

4. When the major symptoms of schizophrenia subside, and the person no longer meets criteria for a formal diagnosis, they are then
      a. diagnosed with the same subtype of schizophrenia, but with a higher global assessment of functioning.
      b. labeled with residual schizophrenia.
      c. frequently diagnosed with major depression.
      d. labeled with undifferentiated schizophrenia.

* 5. Psychotic symptoms, which persist for only three months, would be classified in DSM-IV as
      a. schizotypal personality disorder.
      b. schizophreniform disorder.
      c. schizophrenia.
      d. brief psychotic disorder.

6. Results from molecular genetics studies
      a. have indicated that the schizophrenia gene is located only on chromosome 5.
      b. have indicated that schizophrenia genes are located on chromosomes 1, 5, 6 and 22.
      c. are too varied to make any firm conclusions.
      d. have indicated that schizophrenia is probably transmitted by a single gene.

7. Dopamine receptors appear responsible for
      a. primarily positive symptoms.
      b. primarily negative symptoms.
      c. the onset, but not the maintenance, of schizophrenia.
      d. the maintenance, but not the onset, of schizophrenia.

8.   The sociogenic hypothesis is one attempt to explain why people with schizophrenia
      a. are typically poor.
      b. become violent.
      c. often come from disturbed families.
      d. adjust poorly outside hospitals.

9.   Treatment with Haldol (an antipsychotic drug)
      a. improves both positive and negative symptoms.
      b. improves only positive symptoms.
      c. improves only negative symptoms.
      d. has no effect on either positive or negative symptoms: it targets disorganized speech.

10.   Recent research suggests that cognitive behavioral therapy
      a. is ineffective for people with schizophrenia.
      b. is effective only in reducing positive symptoms, not negative symptoms.
      c. is effective in helping some people with schizophrenia challenge their maladaptive beliefs.
      d. is only effective when used in conjunction with social-skills training.

Short Answer

1.   What diagnosis is appropriate for Russell? He believes he has the instant answer to all the country's problems. When people avoid him (because he constantly lectures them on the topic), he decides they fear the president will hear his ideas and instantly implement them. The president happened to be in town, and Russell walked in assuming the president had come specifically to see him. When body guards threw him out, Russell became irate and declared the president was having sex with his wife and, thus, had refused to see him.

2.   Describe the data which most convincingly point to genetic factors in the etiology of schizophrenia.

3.   Explain how different neural pathways could result in both positive and negative symptoms in current dopamine theory.

4.   Describe two weaknesses of current dopamine theory.

5.   Research indicates that schizophrenics have enlarged ventricles. What does this mean about their brains?

6.   Summarize data suggesting that viral infections contribute to cortical changes in schizophrenia.

7. Explain what the text means in saying that the relation between schizophrenia and social class involves a sharp upturn.

8. In studying developmental factors in schizophrenia, how are most studies limited, and how do high-risk studies help?

9. What is the issue regarding antipsychotic drugs and ethnic minorities?

10. What do "case managers" do in treating schizophrenia, and why are they helpful?

Internet Resources

The following are internet resources to begin exploring the topics in this chapter. Additional general internet resources are at the end of the introduction chapter.

National Alliance for the Mentally Ill (NAMI) is a nonprofit, grassroots, self-help, support, and advocacy organization of consumers, families, and friends of people with severe mental illnesses, such as schizophrenia.

www.nami.org

Schizophrenia.com is a non-profit web community providing in-depth information, support, and education related to schizophrenia.

www.schizophrenia.com

Answers to Self-Test, Chapter 11

Multiple Choice

1. d (p. 350)   2. c (p. 351)   3. c (p. 354)   4. b (p. 358)
5. b (p. 358)   6. b (p. 362)   7. a (p. 364)   8. a (p. 368)
9. b (p. 373-375)   10. c (p. 380)

Short Answer

1. Paranoid schizophrenia. (p. 358)

2. Adoptee studies which indicate high rates of schizophrenia in children of schizophrenic mothers even though the children were raised by others. Family and twin studies are not as convincing. (p. 361)

3. Dopamine neurons in the prefrontal cortex may be underactive resulting in negative symptoms. Additionally, they normally inhibit dopamine neurons in the limbic area. If they are underactive, they may fail to inhibit the limbic area resulting in positive symptoms. (p. 363-364)

4. a) Drugs block dopamine receptors rapidly, but take weeks to become effective, and b) simply reducing dopamine to normal levels is not, typically, sufficient; rather it must be reduced to below normal producing Parkinsonian side effects. (p. 364-365)

5. If ventricles (natural openings in the brain) are enlarged, then the brain has shrunk with loss of brain cells or cell connections. (p. 365-366)

6. Schizophrenia was more common in people whose mothers were exposed to the influenza virus during their second trimester of pregnancy. (p. 367)

7. Schizophrenia is decidedly (not just relatively) more common in the lowest social classes. The rate of schizophrenia is twice as high in the poorest groups compared to next poorest. (p. 368-369)

8. Most data were not collected to study schizophrenia. High-risk studies specifically study childhood variables in people who later develop schizophrenia. (Note that the high-risk method is needed to make such studies practical, as schizophrenia is so generally uncommon.) (p. 371-372)

9. Newer atypical antipsychotics are less often prescribed for ethnic minorities despite the fact that they are generally more effective and that African Americans may be more likely to have side-effects from traditional antipsychotics. (p. 377)

10. They coordinate the services provided by a team and others in the community. Research shows that intensive and coordinated community services reduce hospitalization costs and improve adjustment in many areas. (p. 382)

12 Personality Disorders

Overview

The previous chapter covered schizophrenia and the complex research into it. This chapter and the following one, discuss disorders that have been less widely studied, in part because individuals with these problems often do not seek treatment.

Chapter 12 discusses personality disorders in which people exhibit long-term patterns of thought and behavior that are ineffective, maladaptive, or socially unacceptable. Examples include social withdrawal, self-centeredness, and criminal activity. Chapter 13 will deal with problematic sexual behaviors. These include sexual disorders or deviations, such as fetishism and rape, as well as sexual dysfunctions or inadequacies such as impotence.

Many of the problems in these chapters are characterized by socially disapproved behaviors. Often others want the person to change more than the person does. This raises difficult issues: can (or should) psychologists change people who do not especially seek change? Are psychologists acting as helpers, as law enforcers, or as moral authorities? Such issues are difficult to answer.

After Chapter 13, the next two chapters cover disorders and issues of childhood (Chapter 14) and old age (Chapter 15). They will complete the text's discussion of psychological disorders. In Chapters 16 and 17, the text will turn to general issues in abnormal psychology.

Chapter Summary

Coded on Axis II in DSM-IV-TR, personality disorders are defined as enduring patterns of behavior and inner experience that disrupt functioning. Personality disorders are grouped into three clusters in DSM-IV-TR: odd/eccentric, dramatic/erratic, and anxious/fearful.

Personality disorders are usually comorbid with such Axis I disorders as depression and anxiety disorders and tend to predict poorer outcomes for these disorders.

The high comorbidity of personality disorders with each other, the difficulties in reliably determining when a person meets diagnostic criteria, and the fact that personality disorders are seen as the extremes of continuously distributed personality traits, has led to proposals to develop a dimensional, rather than a categorical, means of classifying these disorders.

The Odd/Eccentric Cluster   Specific diagnoses in the odd/eccentric cluster include paranoid, schizoid, and schizotypal.

The major symptom of paranoid personality disorder is suspiciousness and mistrust; of schizoid personality disorder, interpersonal detachment; and of schizotypal personality disorder, unusual thought and behavior.

Behavior-genetic research supports the idea that schizotypal personality disorder is related to schizophrenia.

The Dramatic/Erratic Cluster   The dramatic/erratic cluster includes borderline, histrionic, narcissistic, and antisocial personality disorders.

The major symptom of borderline personality disorder is unstable, highly changeable emotion and behavior; of histrionic personality disorder, exaggerated emotional displays; and of narcissistic personality disorder, highly inflated self-esteem.   Antisocial personality disorder and psychopathy overlap a great deal, but are not equivalent.   The diagnosis of antisocial personality focuses on behavior, whereas that of psychopathy emphasizes emotional deficits.

There is evidence that much of the vulnerability to borderline personality disorder is inherited, and there are also (somewhat inconsistent) findings regarding deficits in frontal lobe functioning and greater amygdala activation.

Psychosocial theories of the etiology of borderline, histrionic, and narcissistic disorders focus on early parent-child relationships.   It is clear that people with borderline personality disorder report extremely high rates of child abuse and parental separation compared to the general population.

The object-relations theorist, Kernberg, and the self-psychologist, Kohut, have detailed proposals concerning borderline and narcissistic personality disorders, focusing on the child developing an insecure ego because of inconsistent love and attention from the parents.   Linehan's cognitive behavioral theory of borderline personality disorder proposes an interaction between a deficit in emotional regulation and an invalidating family environment.

A predisposition to antisocial personality disorder and psychopathy is inherited.

Psychopaths tend to have fathers who were antisocial.   During their childhood discipline was often absent or inconsistent.

The core problem of the psychopath, however, might be that impending punishment creates no inhibitions about committing antisocial acts.   A lack of empathy might also be a factor in the psychopath's callous treatment of others.

The Anxious/Fearful Cluster   The anxious/fearful cluster includes avoidant, dependent, and obsessive-compulsive personality disorders.

The major symptom of avoidant personality disorder is fear of rejection or criticism; of dependent personality disorder, low self-confidence; and of obsessive-compulsive personality disorder, a perfectionistic, detail-oriented style.

Theories of etiology for the anxious/fearful cluster focus on early experience.   Avoidant personality disorder might result from the transmission of fear from parent to child via modeling.   Dependent personality might be caused by disruptions of the parent-child relationship (e.g., through separation or loss) that lead the person to fear losing other relationships in adulthood.   It is important to note that dependency as a personality trait is at least partially inherited.

Treatments   Although psychodynamic, behavioral and cognitive, and pharmacological treatments are all used for personality disorders, less research has been conducted for these disorders compared to Axis I disorders.

Several medications appear to be helpful for quelling specific symptoms.

Early research on day treatment programs is promising.

Some promising evidence is emerging for the utility of dialectical behavior therapy for borderline personality disorder. This approach combines client-centered acceptance with a cognitive behavioral focus on making specific changes in thought, emotion, and behavior. Recent research suggests that even psychopathy, often considered virtually untreatable, might respond to intensive psychological treatment.

Learning Goals

1. Be able to explain the key features of each personality disorder, the issues in classifying these disorders, and alternative dimensional approaches to diagnosis.

2. Be able to describe the genetic, neurobiological, social-environmental, and other risk factors for personality disorders, and be able to discuss problems in the research on etiology.

3. Be able to describe the available medication and psychological treatments of personality disorders.

Key Terms

Personality disorders (p. 387)

Five-factor model (p. 390)

Paranoid personality disorder (p. 391)

Schizoid personality disorder (p. 392)

Schizotypal personality disorder (p. 392)

Borderline personality disorder (p. 394)

Object-relations theory (p. 395-396)

Histrionic personality disorder (p. 396)

Narcissistic personality disorder (p. 397)

Antisocial personality disorder (p. 399)

Psychopathy (p. 399)

Avoidant personality disorder (p. 403)

Dependent personality disorder (p. 404)

Obsessive-compulsive personality disorder (p. 405)

Dialectical behavior therapy (p. 409)

Study Questions

1. Define personality disorders as a group. How are they different from normal personality styles? (p. 387)

Classifying Personality Disorders (p. 388-391)

2. Describe two problems with the DSM approach to personality disorders. Describe an alternative, five-factor approach. Identify several possible advantages and problems with the five-factor approach. (p. 388-391)

Odd/Eccentric Cluster (p. 391-393)

3.   Identify and briefly describe the three disorders in the odd/eccentric cluster. Be able to distinguish them from each other and from similar Axis I disorders. What is known about their etiology (and why is it hard to study them)? (p. 391-393)

Dramatic/Erratic Cluster (p. 393-403)

4.   Why has borderline personality disorder been a major focus of interest? Describe the characteristics of borderline personality disorder. Summarize four views on its etiology. (p. 394-396)

5.   Describe the characteristics of Histrionic Personality Disorder and one theory of its etiology. Describe the characteristics of Narcissistic Personality Disorder and two theories of its etiology. (p. 396-398)

6.   Define and distinguish between the terms "antisocial personality disorder" and "psychopathy". Summarize three controversies regarding the DSM approach. List two issues that complicate research on antisocial personality disorder and psychopathy. (p. 398-400)

7.   What genetic and family environmental factors are involved in antisocial personality disorder and psychopathy? Summarize research in three areas indicating little anxiety in psychopaths and one area indicating little empathy. Also, summarize research on response modulation indicating that psychopaths respond impulsively. (p. 400-403)

Anxious/Fearful Cluster (p. 403-406)

8.   Briefly describe the three disorders in the anxious/fearful cluster. (Note how obsessive-compulsive personality disorder is different from obsessive-compulsive disorder.) Give a speculated cause for each of the three disorders. (p. 403-406)

Treatment of Personality Disorders (p. 406-412)

9.   Why is treatment of personality disorders difficult? Identify three methods of treatment. In general, how do therapists of various paradigms approach working with personality disorders? Explain the idea that therapy with personality disorders seeks to change a "disorder" into a "style". (p. 406-408)

10.   Give two reasons that therapy with borderline personalities is especially difficult.   Describe two approaches to therapy for borderline personalities. (p. 408-411)

11.   What is the traditional view on treatment of psychopathy? Summarize recent meta-analyses suggesting more optimism. (p. 411)

Self-Test, Chapter 12

(* Items not covered in Study Questions.)

Multiple Choice

1. Personality disorders differ from normal personality in that
    a. personality disorders are short-term difficulties while personality is life-long.
    b. personality disorders represent the extremes of normal personality variables.
    c. personality disorders have an antisocial component.
    d. all of the above choices are correct.

2. The personality traits tapped by the DSM-IV personality disorders category
    a. are categorical; that is, a person either has or does not have the trait in question.
    b. are situational; that is, they are thought to exist only in a limited set of circumstances.
    c. form a continuum; that is, they are present to varying degrees in almost everyone.
    d. are very rare; that is, most people do not exhibit them.

3. Clarita has very few friends and does not wish to make more friends. She appears indifferent to other people, aloof, and a loner. Which of the following personality disorders is the best diagnosis for Clarita?
    a. schizoid
    b. schizotypal
    c. narcissistic
    d. avoidant

4. Impulsivity and rapidly changeable beliefs, emotions, and relationships are characteristic of _____personality disorder.
    a. narcissistic
    b. schizoid
    c. antisocial
    d. borderline

5. Linehan's theory of borderline personality disorder is
    a. biological.
    b. environmental.
    c. social.
    d. both biological and environmental.

6. Cleckley emphasized which of the following aspects of antisocial personality that is not emphasized in DSM-IV?
    a. acting out as a child
    b. lack of shame and positive emotions
    c. reckless and aggressive
    d. impulsive antisocial acts

7. Adoption research suggests that
    a. there is little relation between heritability and antisocial personality.
    b. adoptive parents sometimes behave in harsh ways due to the child's genetically influenced antisocial difficult behavior.
    c. adoptive parents insulate a genetically at-risk child from psychopathy.
    d. none of the above choices are correct.

8. Which is the most appropriate label for Professor Crawford? He tries so hard to teach well that he never finishes the course syllabus. His lectures and tests focus on detailed information and being correct, but rarely address overriding current issues in the field.
    a. borderline personality disorder
    b. histrionic personality disorder
    c. schizotypal personality disorder
    d. obsessive-compulsive personality disorder

9. Behavior and cognitive therapists have generally treated most forms of personality disorder by
    a. redefining the problem in more specific terms.
    b. doing cognitive therapy that emphasizes that behavior is state-like and not trait-like.
    c. using money as a reinforcer to shape socially desirable behavior.
    d. working with teachers as a prevention measure for future instances of personality disorders.

10. Psychopaths typically do <u>not</u> benefit from psychotherapy because
    a. their cognitive functioning is often too low.
    b. they have a limited capacity for psychological insight.
    c. they often "play along" with the therapist.
    d. all of the above choices are correct.

Short Answer

1. Define "personality disorders" as a group.

2. According to research, what are the limitations of the five-factor approach?

3. Distinguish between schizoid and schizotypal personality disorders.

4. Summarize the psychoanalytic theory of the origins of histrionic personality disorder.

5. Research shows that psychopaths tend to come from families marked by what characteristics?

6. Describe research on response modulation showing impulsivity in psychopaths.

7. What is the (speculated) cause of obsessive-compulsive personality disorder?

8.   Marco seeks psychotherapeutic help. It's clear that he has a personality disorder as well as an Axis I problem. What is the therapeutic implication of his also having an Axis II diagnosis?

9.   What does it mean to say that the goal of therapy should be to change disorders into styles?

10.   Describe the basic approach of dialectical behavior therapy for borderline personality disorder.

Internet Resources

The following are Internet resources to begin exploring the topics in this chapter. Additional general Internet resources are at the end of the introduction chapter.

BPD Central provides resources for people who have a loved one with borderline personality disorder.   www.bpdcentral.com

Personality Disorders Foundation provides information to researchers, students, and the public including links to many other websites.   pdf.uchc.edu

Answers to Self-Test, Chapter 12

Multiple Choice

1. b (p. 387)   2. c (p. 390)   3. a (p. 392)   4. d (p. 394)
5. d (p. 396)   6. b (p. 399-400)   7. b (p. 401)   8. d (p. 405)
9. a (p. 407)   10. c (p. 411)

Short Answer

1. Characterized by enduring, inflexible patterns of inner experience and behavior that deviate from cultural expectations and cause distress or impairment. (p. 387)

2. Many personality disorders showed similar profiles (which may suggest the need for a more detailed analysis of facets). A few disorders appear qualitatively different suggesting a categorical difference. (p. 390-391)

3. Both have few close friends but schizotypal personality disorder also involves eccentric ideas, mannerisms, appearance, etc. (p. 392-393)

4. The person grew up with parents who seemed preoccupied by sex, but described it as dirty. Thus they learned to seek attention by being sexy and emotional while avoiding intimacy and sexuality. (p. 397-398)

5. Inconsistent discipline, negativity, lack of affection, marital problems, substance abuse, and antisocial fathers. (p. 401)

6. In a card game where the odds of winning decreased steadily, psychopaths continued to play (and lose) longer than others, unless they were required to wait 5 seconds before deciding whether to continue. (p. 402)

7. They are overcompensating for fear of loss of control by pushing to control as much of their life as possible. (p. 405)

8. Implication is that therapy will take longer and the outcome is less optimistic as Marco has both an acute problem and an underlying, long-term, problem. (p. 406-407)

9. The goal should be not to change the person's basic approach to life but to help the person express it in more adaptive, moderate, flexible ways. (p. 407-408)

10. Therapist combines client-centered and behavioral approaches. The client feels accepted as he/she really is yet helped to change problematic behaviors. By combining these seeming opposites, the therapist helps the client see that the world is not black or white, but is both (synthesis). (p. 409)

13 Sexual and Gender Identity Disorders

Overview

Chapter 13 is the second of two chapters on problems with a social emphasis. Generally, these are not considered "mental illnesses" as such, but involve particular behaviors or traits that are of concern to society and, sometimes, to the individual. Chapter 12 discussed personality disorders. Many personality disorders, especially antisocial personality disorder, are clearly more a "problem" for society than for the individual involved.

Chapter 13 covers sexual problems in which social concerns are also prominent. Sexual deviations, as the term implies, refer to sexual activities that society considers deviant or aberrant. Like the personality disorders in the last chapter, defining a sexual activity as "deviant" involves a value judgment. Social and individual values may change as is happening regarding homosexuality. Sexual dysfunctions are much more common sexual problems involving inhibitions of sexual functioning. Sexual dysfunctions include premature orgasm, vaginismus, and inhibited sexual desire or arousal. Sexual dysfunctions are frustrating to the individual and hamper relationships.

Chapter 13 is the last chapter focusing on socially problematic behaviors. The next two chapters discuss issues and problems of childhood (Chapter 15) and of old age (Chapter 16). Then the text concludes with two chapters on treatment and on legal/ethical issues.

Chapter Summary

Sexual Norms Sexual behavior and attitudes are heavily influenced by culture, and so any discussion of disorders in sexuality must be sensitive to the idea that norms are likely to change over time and place. Currently, a great deal of research is focused on gender differences in sexuality.

Sexual Dysfunctions The DSM categorizes these disturbances in four groups: sexual desire disorders, sexual arousal disorders, orgasmic disorders, and sexual pain disorders. Many people experience brief sexual symptoms, but these are not diagnosable unless they are recurrent, cause either distress or impairment, and are not explained by medical conditions.

Research on the etiology of sexual dysfunctions is difficult to conduct, as surveys may be inaccurate, and laboratory measures may be difficult to gather. Researchers have identified many different variables that can contribute to sexual dysfunctions, including biological variables, previous sexual experiences, relationship issues, psychopathology, affect and arousal, and negative cognitions.

Many effective interventions for sexual dysfunctions are available, many of them cognitive behavioral. Sex therapy, aimed at reversing old habits and teaching new skills, was propelled into public consciousness by the Masters and Johnson work. Their method hinges on gradual, nonthreatening exposure to increasingly intimate sexual encounters and the sanctioning of sexuality by credible and sensitive therapists. Sex therapists also aim to educate patients in sexual anatomy and physiology, reduce anxiety, teach communication skills, and improve attitudes and thoughts about sexuality. Couples therapy is sometimes appropriate as well. Biological treatments such as Viagra may also be used, especially when the sexual dysfunction is primarily due to physical rather than psychological causes, as in many cases of erectile dysfunction.

Gender Identity Disorder   Gender identity disorder (GID) involves the deep and persistent conviction of the person that his or her anatomic sexual makeup and psychological sense of self as male or female are discrepant. Thus, a man with GID is physically male, but considers himself a woman and desires to live as a woman.

Neurobiological models of GID emphasize genes and prenatal hormone exposure. Research on neurobiology, though, has typically focused on sex-typed behavior and attitudes, rather than full-blown diagnoses, and even then, neurobiological variables account for only a certain amount of the variance. Another theory proposes that parents may have reinforced cross-gender behavior. This theory has been criticized though, as most children who show cross-gender behaviors are harshly criticized by peers.

The most common treatment for GID is sex-reassignment surgery to bring bodily features into line with gender identity. There are case reports that behavioral treatment can help a person minimize cross-gender behavior.

Paraphilias   In the paraphilias, unusual imagery and acts are persistent and necessary for sexual gratification. The principal paraphilias are fetishism, transvestic fetishism, pedophilia, voyeurism, exhibitionism, frotteurism, sexual sadism, and sexual masochism.

Efforts have also been made to detect hormonal anomalies in people with paraphilias, but the findings are inconclusive.

According to the psychodynamic view, the person with a paraphilia is fearful of conventional heterosexual relationships; there is no empirical support for this idea. One behavioral view is that a fetishistic attraction to objects arises from accidental classical conditioning of sexual arousal, but this view has not received much empirical support. Another behavioral hypothesis posits deficiencies in social skills that make it difficult for the person to interact normally with other adults, but again, there is limited support for this idea. Cognitive distortions appear to be involved.

The most promising treatments for the paraphilias are cognitive behavioral. One conditioning procedure is to pair the inappropriate sexual object with painful or aversive events. Cognitive methods focus on the cognitive distortions of the person with a paraphilia; social-skills and empathy training are also common. A range of studies suggest that psychological treatments do reduce the number of legal offenses. SSRIs and drugs that reduce testosterone levels have both been found to reduce sex drive and deviant sexual behaviors, but because of the side effects, there are ethical issues involved in the use of these drugs.

Rape   Rape, although it is not separately diagnosed in DSM-IV-TR, results in considerable psychological trauma for the victim and is far too prevalent. Some estimates suggest that 20-25% of women will be raped during their lifetime. The nature of rapes vary a great deal; some people rape strangers, but most rapes are committed by someone known to the woman. The inclusion of rape in a discussion of human sexuality is a matter of some controversy, as many theorists regard rape as an act of aggressive violence rather than of sex.

Although there is no single profile that fits all rapists, variables that appear to distinguish rapists include high levels of hostility towards women, antisocial and impulsive personality traits, and high rates of sexual dysfunction. Social skills do not seem to be poor, except for in convicted rapists. Many have emphasized that the likelihood of rape is likely to be higher in societies that condone interpersonal violence.

Psychological treatment programs focus on increasing empathy for victims, anger management, self-esteem, and substance abuse. Biological treatments, like those used for paraphilias, are used to decrease sex drive by lowering male hormone levels. Treatment has been shown to reduce the rate of recidivism. A major concern is that most rapes do not get reported to police, and so few rapists are convicted.

Learning Goals

1.   Be able to describe norms and gender differences in sexuality.

2.   Be able to define the phases of the sexual response cycle.

3.   Be able to explain the symptoms, causes, and treatments for sexual dysfunctions, gender identity disorder, and paraphilias.

4.   Be able to discuss the epidemiology and predictors of rape and sexual coercion, as well as treatment programs for sexual offenders.

Key Terms

Sexual dysfunctions (p. 413)

Gender identity disorder (p. 414)

Paraphilias (p. 414)

Sexual response cycle (p. 416)

Appetitive phase (p. 416)

Excitement phase (p. 416)

Orgasm phase (p. 416)

Resolution phase (p. 416)

Hypoactive sexual desire disorder (p. 419)

Sexual aversion disorder (p. 419)

Female sexual arousal disorder (p. 420)

Male erectile disorder (p. 420)

Female orgasmic disorder (p. 420)

Male orgasmic disorder (p. 420)

Premature ejaculation (p. 420)

Dyspareunia (p. 421)

Vaginismus (p. 421)

Spectator role (p. 421)

Penile plethysmograph (p. 423)

Sensate focus (p. 425)

Gender identity (p. 428)

Sexual orientation (p. 428)

Sex-reassignment surgery (p. 431)

Paraphilias (p. 433)

Fetishism (p. 433)

Transvestic fetishism (p. 434)

Pedophilia (p. 434)

Incest (p. 435)

Voyeurism (p. 435-436)

Childhood sexual abuse [CSA] (p. 436)

Exhibitionism (p. 437)

Frotteurism (p. 438)

Sexual sadism (p. 438)

Sexual masochism (p. 438)

Forced rape (p. 444)

Statutory rape (p. 444)

Study Questions

1. Identify and distinguish among the three kinds of sexual problems discussed in this chapter. (p. 413)

Sexual Norms and Behavior (p. 413-417)

2.   Illustrate how sexual norms have changed over time. Describe the four phases of the sexual response cycle noting gender difference in the resolution phase. (p. 413-417)

Sexual Dysfunctions (p. 417-428)

3.   How common are occasional disturbances in sexual functioning, and when are they labeled as dysfunctions?   Describe nine sexual dysfunctions organized into four categories. (Note the parallels between these categories and the phases of the sexual response cycle.) (p. 417-421)

4.   Summarize Masters and Johnson's view of the etiology of sexual dysfunctions.   Illustrate the wide range of biological and psychosocial factors in sexual dysfunctions. Briefly describe eight techniques for treating sexual dysfunctions (noting that they are often combined in practice). (p. 421-428)

Gender Identity Disorder (p. 428-432)

5.   Define gender identity disorder (GID) distinguishing it from sexual orientation. Give three reasons its inclusion in DSM is controversial.   Summarize evidence that genetic, neurobiological, and psychosocial factors may be involved (while noting the limits of these studies). (p. 428-431)

6.   Describe the steps in treating GID by altering the body.   How effective is this treatment? Describe behavioral treatments to alter gender identity and reasons to be skeptical about the results. (p. 431-432)

The Paraphilias (p. 433-443)

7.   Define paraphilias as a group of disorders.   Define eight paraphilias and any special issues associated with each. (p. 433-439)

8. Why is there little research on the etiology of paraphilias? Summarize one neurbiological, one psychodynamic, and three psychological possibilities (p. 439-440)

9. Why is it difficult to study treatment of paraphilias in terms of research dilemmas and the people themselves?   Give several examples of two cognitive behavioral approaches and describe current broader programs. Describe three biological treatments and issues in their use. Describe Megan's Law as a preventive measure. (p. 440-443)

Rape (p. 444-447)

10. How common is rape, especially on college campuses?   Is rape a sexual crime? Explain. Identify common characteristics of rapists. Describe psychological treatment of rapists and its effectiveness. Explain the need to reform the legal system's approach to rape. (p. 444-447)

Self-Test, Chapter 13

(* Items not covered in Study Questions.)

Multiple Choice

* 1. Which of the following statements is correct?
    a. Women develop more sexual dysfunctions as they age.
    b. Women are more likely to desire sex more often and desire more sexual partners.
    c. Women report more engagement in sexual thought and behavior than men.
    d. Men report more engagement in sexual thought and behavior than women.

2. Elizabeth is beginning to feel aroused from direct physical contact with her husband. She is thinking about what it will be like to have intercourse with him. Masters and Johnson describe this as the
    a. arousal mechanism.
    b. excitement phase.
    c. appetitive response.
    d. fantasy period.

3. The following DSM-IV-TR diagnosis has historically been associated with the derogatory label of 'frigidity.'
    a. female orgasmic disorder
    b. dyspareunia
    c. sexual aversion disorder
    d. female sexual arousal disorder

4. Which of the following are the two orgasmic disorders of men in the DSM-IV?
    a. male orgasmic disorder and premature ejaculation
    b. premature ejaculation and sexual aversion disorder
    c. dyspareunia and male orgasmic disorder
    d. premature ejaculation and vaginismus

5. The term "spectator role" refers to
    a. the disengaged father in a family system.
    b. the experience of a person with speech anxiety while preparing for a speech.
    c. a detached state of mind during sexual intercourse.
    d. people who fail to help a crime victim because of not wanting to get involved.

6. Which of the following is not an approach used to treat sexual dysfunction?
    a. anxiety reduction
    b. directed masturbation
    c. skills and communication training
    d. personal therapy

7. A variable that appears correlated with gender identity disorder is
    a. reinforcement of cross-dressing incidents in childhood.
    b. paternal gender identity disorder.
    c. attractiveness of the child.
    d. ratio of same-sex to opposite-sex friends during early childhood.

8.   When people derive sexual gratification from rubbing their genitals on an unsuspecting
      individual, they would be diagnosed with
      a. exhibitionism.
      b. frotteurism.
      c. sadism.
      d. voyeurism.

9.   Contemporary biological therapy for sex offenders may involve
      a. removal of primary sex organs.
      b. administration of strong tranquilizing agents.
      c. administration of drugs that reduce androgen levels.
      d. delivery of antidepressant drugs by injection.

* 10. The former label ego-dystonic homosexuality involved a logical contradiction by implying that
      homosexuals
      a. could not be treated.
      b. also had heterosexual impulses.
      c. were not disturbed.
      d. were abnormal only if they were persuaded by social prejudice.

Short Answer

1.   In general, what are the distinctions among the three kinds of sexual disorders described in the
      chapter?

2.   Illustrate how sexual norms have changed over recent centuries.

3.   Give three reasons that including gender identity disorder in DSM is controversial.

4.   Describe the steps in changing the body to treat gender identity disorder.

5.   Why should we be skeptical of studies of behavioral treatments to alter gender identity?

6.   Mike often wears skirts. What else do we need to know in order to label Mike?

7.   Summarize three hypothesized psychological factors in the etiology of paraphilias.

8.   Give two reasons why it is difficult to study the treatment of paraphilias.

9.   Summarize the rationale for saying that rape is not a sexual crime.

10.   Explain the need to reform the legal system's approach to rape.

Internet Resources

The following are Internet resources to begin exploring the topics in this chapter. Additional general Internet resources are at the end of the introduction chapter.

Female Sexual Dysfunction: Evaluation and Treatment is a comprehensive, medically-oriented review.   www.aafp.org/afp/20000701/127.html

Psychology of Gender Identity and Transgenderism is written by a transgendered psychologist.
                                                                www.genderpsychology.org

Answers to Self-Test, Chapter 13

Multiple Choice

1. d (p. 414)	2. b (p. 416)	3. d (p. 420)	4. a (p. 420)
5. c (p. 421)	6. d (p. 424-427)	7. a (p. 429)	8. b (p. 438)
9. c (p. 443)	10. d (p. 415)		

Short Answer

1. Sexual dysfunctions involve normal sexual activities. Paraphilias involve unusual or inappropriate sexual activities. Gender identity disorder involves inner beliefs (not activities). (p. 413)

2. In the late 1800s and early 1900s, sex was to be restrained as harmful or weakening the body. Today sex is often considered desirable or a right as illustrated by Internet pornography and Viagra sales. (p. 413-414)

3. a) including GID may legitimatize current social prejudice, b) diversity in gender roles and behavior is widespread in humans and animals, and c) GID lacks predictive value as many children cross-dress, but outgrow it. (p. 429)

4. First, the person is asked to live as the other gender for 6 to 12 months. Psychotherapy helps in the adjustment. Physical procedures help alter body image such as hormones and cosmetic surgery. Finally sex–reassignment surgery is done to alter genitalia. (p. 431-432)

5. Most people with gender identity disorder reject this option. Thus, the few reported attempts (while successful) were not on people not typical of people with GID. (p. 432)

6. We need to know how Mike sees his gender. If he sees himself as female, the label is gender identity disorder. If he sees himself as male, the label is transvestic fetishism. (p. 434)

7. a) classical conditioning of sexual arousal to inappropriate stimuli, b) poor social skills that limit appropriate sexual contacts, perhaps resulting from poor parent-child relationships, and c) cognitive distortions about the act and/or others. (p. 440)

8. Because most paraphilias are illegal a) researchers are reluctant to include no-treatment control groups, and b) many sex offenders are court-ordered into treatment and minimally motivated to change. (p. 440)

9. Calling it a sexual crime masks the violent nature of the act and encourages questioning the sexual motives and background of the victim. (p. 445)

10. Many rape victims are reluctant to report the crime fearing reprisals and police insensitivity. Trials are often stressful for the victim and convictions are uncommon despite some recent reforms. (p. 447)

14 Disorders of Childhood

Overview

Chapter 13 concluded two chapters on socially problematic behaviors and traits. This is the first of two chapters devoted to developmental problems and issues. Chapter 14 covers issues and problems that arise in childhood; Chapter 15 covers issues and problems of old age. Both chapters focus on special issues of young/old people in our society, as well as on their psychological problems.

Disorders of childhood (in this chapter) are complicated by several factors. Children are developing and changing rapidly. They have difficulty expressing their concerns or asking for help. Not surprisingly, the help they receive is, often, for problems that bother the adults around them. Typically, these include misbehavior (hyperactivity and conduct disorders) and educational difficulties (learning disabilities and mental retardation). Chapter 14 also covers childhood autism, a serious and pervasive developmental problem.

The next chapter, Chapter 15, will deal with problems of aging. Older individuals are subject to a wide variety of problems. They must cope with deterioration, as well as whatever problems they may have developed over time. More importantly, they must cope with the realization that they are getting older as well as the fact that society often does not seem to respect, value, or provide for them.

Chapters 14 and 15 complete the text's discussion of specific problems. The last chapters of the text focus on other issues related to abnormal psychology. Chapter 16 discusses issues in psychological intervention. Chapter 17 covers legal and ethical issues. Such issues have been mentioned throughout the text, but these last two chapters provide a more organized and extensive discussion of them.

Chapter Summary

Clinical Descriptions Childhood disorders are often organized into two domains: externalizing disorders and internalizing disorders. Externalizing disorders are characterized by such behaviors as aggressiveness, noncompliance, overactivity, and impulsiveness; they include attention-deficit/hyperactivity disorder, conduct disorder, and oppositional defiant disorder. Internalizing disorders are characterized by such behaviors as depression, social withdrawal, and anxiety and include childhood anxiety and mood disorders.

Attention-deficit/hyperactivity disorder (ADHD) is a persistent pattern of inattention and/or hyperactivity and impulsivity that is more frequent and more severe than what is typically observed in children of a given age. Conduct disorder is sometimes a precursor to antisocial personality disorder in adulthood, though many children carrying the diagnosis do not progress to that extreme. It is characterized by high and widespread levels of aggression, lying, theft, vandalism, cruelty to other people and to animals, and other acts that violate laws and social norms.

Mood and anxiety disorders in children share similarities with the adult forms of these disorders. However, differences that reflect different stages of development are also important.

Learning disorders are diagnosed when a child fails to develop to the degree expected for his or her intellectual level in a specific academic, language, or motor-skill area. These disorders are often identified and treated within the school system rather than through mental health clinics.

The DSM-IV-TR diagnostic criteria for mental retardation are subaverage intellectual functioning and deficits in adaptive behavior, with onset before the age of eighteen. Most professionals, however, focus more on the strengths of individuals with mental retardation than on their assignment to a particular level of severity. This shift in emphasis is associated with increased efforts to design psychological and educational interventions that make the most of individuals' abilities.

Autistic disorder, one of the pervasive developmental disorders, begins before the age of two and a half. The major symptoms are a failure to relate to other people; communication problems, consisting of either a failure to learn any language or speech irregularities, such as echolalia and pronoun reversal; and theory of mind problems.

Etiology There is strong evidence for genetic and neurobiological factors in the etiology of ADHD. Low birth weight and maternal smoking are also risk factors. Family factors interact with these genetic vulnerabilities.

Among the apparent etiological and risk factors for Conduct Disorder are a genetic predisposition, inadequate learning of moral awareness, modeling and direct reinforcement of antisocial behavior, negative peer influences, and living in impoverished and crime-ridden areas.

Etiological factors for mood and anxiety disorders in children are believed to be the same as in adulthood, though additional research is needed.

There is mounting evidence that the most widely studied of the learning disorders, dyslexia, has genetic and other neurobiological components.

The more severe forms of mental retardation have a neurological basis, such as the chromosomal trisomy that causes Down syndrome. Certain infectious diseases in the pregnant mother, such as HIV, rubella, and syphilis, as well as illnesses that affect the child directly, such as encephalitis, can stunt cognitive and social development, as can malnutrition, severe falls, and automobile accidents that injure the brain. Environmental factors are considered the principal causes of milder mental retardation.

Family and twin studies give compelling evidence of a genetic predisposition. Abnormalities have been found in the brains of autistic children, including an overgrowth of the brain by age 2 and abnormalities in the cerebellum.

Treatment A combined treatment including stimulant drugs, such as Ritalin, and reinforcement for staying on task has shown effectiveness in reducing the symptoms of ADHD.

The most promising approach to treating young people with conduct disorder involves intensive intervention in multiple systems, including the family, school, and peer systems.

The most effective interventions for mood and anxiety disorders are cognitive-behavioral therapy. Medication is effective for depression among adolescents, though its use is not without controversy.

The most widespread interventions for dyslexia are educational.

Many children with mental retardation who would formerly have been institutionalized are now being educated in the public schools under the provisions of Public Law 94-142. In addition, using applied behavioral analysis, self-instructional training, and modeling, behavior therapists have been able to treat successfully many of the behavioral problems of individuals with mental retardation and to improve their intellectual functioning.

The most promising treatments for autism are psychological in nature, involving intensive behavioral interventions and work with parents. Various drug treatments have been used but have proved less effective than behavioral interventions.

Learning Goals

1. Be able to describe the issues in the classification of psychopathology in children

2. Be able to discuss the description, etiology, and treatments for externalizing problems, including ADHD and conduct disorder, and for internalizing problems, including depression and anxiety

3. Be able to distinguish the distinctions between the different learning disabilities as well as our current understanding on the causes and treatments for dyslexia

4. Be able to describe the different systems for classifying mental retardation and the current research on causes and treatments.

5. Be able to describe the symptoms, causes, and treatments for autism and aspergers syndrome.

Key Terms

Developmental psychopathology (p. 450)

Externalizing disorders (p. 451)

Internalizing disorders (p. 451)

Attention-deficit/hyperactivity disorder [ADHD] (p. 451)

Conduct disorder (p. 460)

Oppositional defiant disorder (p. 461)

Parental management training [PMT] (p. 465)

Multisystemic treatment [MST] (p. 467)

School phobia (p. 471)

Learning disability (p. 474)

Learning disorders (p. 474)

Reading disorder [dyslexia] (p. 474)

Disorder of written expression (p. 474)

Mathematics disorder (p. 474)

Communication disorders (p. 474)

Expressive language disorder (p. 474)

Phonological disorder (p. 474-475)

Stuttering (p. 475)

Motor skills disorder (p. 475)

Mental retardation (p. 478)

Down syndrome [trisomy 21] (p. 481)

Fragile X syndrome (p. 481)

Phenylketonuria (p. 481)

Autistic disorder (p. 485)

Pervasive developmental disorders (p. 485)

Rett's disorder (p. 485)

Childhood disintegrative disorder (p. 485)

Asperger's disorder (p. 485)

Echolalia (p. 488)

Pronoun reversal (p. 488)

Study Questions

Classification and Diagnosis of Childhood Disorders (p. 450-451)

1. To classify abnormal behavior in children, what must diagnosticians consider first and why? Define two broad classes into which many childhood disorders are organized. (p. 450-451)

Attention-Deficit/Hyperactivity Disorder (p. 451-460)

2. Distinguish between attention-deficit/hyperactivity disorder (ADHD) and "rambunctious kid". Identify four or so characteristics of ADHD. Identify three subtypes suggesting two disorders. Distinguish between ADHD and conduct disorder. What is the adult prognosis for ADHD children? (p. 451-455)

3.   Describe and evaluate the importance of five etiological factors in hyperactivity. Describe medication treatments for hyperactivity. How important are medications and what is their limitation? Describe psychological treatments and results of studies comparing them and medication. (p. 455-460)

Conduct Disorder (p. 460-468)

4.   Distinguish between conduct disorder and oppositional defiant disorder (ODD). Describe characteristics of conduct disorder. Describe Moffitt's effort to distinguish two prognoses and factors affecting prognosis. (p. 460-463)

5.   Identify important genetic, neurobiological, psychological, peer, and sociological influences in the etiology of conduct disorder. Describe and evaluate treatment approaches based on family intervention, multisystem treatment, and cognitive therapy. (p. 463-468)

Depression and Anxiety in Children and Adolescents (p. 468-473)

6.   Summarize the characteristics, etiology and treatment of depression in children and adolescents noting especially differences between childhood and adult depression.   What is the prognosis for childhood anxiety, and what are two reasons to be concerned about it?   Describe three common childhood anxieties.   Describe two approaches to treatment. (p. 468-473)

Learning disabilities (p. 473-478)

7.   Define seven learning disabilities categorized in three groups.   In the etiology of dyslexia, describe phonological awareness and the kind of studies investigating it in children and in adults.   In the etiology of mathematics disorder, describe three subtypes.   Describe two common approaches to intervention and a common need in any intervention program. (p. 473-478)

Mental Retardation (p. 478-484)

8.   Define "mental retardation" using three traditional criteria.   Explain the idea of levels of retardation in DSM-IV-TR.   Describe the approach encouraged by the American Association of Mental Retardation and the advantages of this approach. (p. 478-480)

9.   In what percentage of cases is there no identified cause of mental retardation? For those with known etiologies, briefly describe five neurobiological causes with one or two examples of each. (p. 481-483)

10.   Describe and evaluate four approaches to treating mental retardation. (p. 483-484)

Autistic Disorder (p. 485-494)

11.   What is considered the fundamental symptom of autistic disorder? Briefly describe three other pervasive developmental disorders in DSM. Describe the characteristics of autism in four areas (about three points for each area). What is the prognosis for autistic children? (p. 485-489)

12.   Summarize early psychological approaches to autism. How well has research supported them?
      How strong are genetic factors in autism? Describe three or so brain abnormalities in autism.
      (p. 489-492)

13.   Describe the method and results of an early behavioral treatment for autism. More generally,
      describe the effects of involving parents and of different strategies for training. How effective
      are medications in treating autism? (p. 492-493)

Self-Test, Chapter 14

(* Items not covered in Study Questions.)

Multiple Choice

1. When diagnosing childhood disorders, it is important to take into account
   a. the potential for lifelong discrimination from being labeled.
   b. differing social expectations as children mature.
   c. the inability of children to verbalize their concerns.
   d. cultural differences in child-rearing practices.

2. The brains of children with ADHD differ from those of normal children in that they have
   a. excessive dopamine activity.
   b. subtle seizure activity in the temporal lobes.
   c. smaller frontal lobes.
   d. None of the above; no differences have been found.

3. Behavioral programs for ADHD children focus on
   a. improving specific social and academic skills.
   b. reducing activity level and restlessness.
   c. calming and relaxing the child.
   d. relieving the side effects of their medication.

4. What is the prognosis for children labeled as having conduct disorder?
   a. The vast majority outgrow their problems naturally.
   b. The vast majority outgrow their problems, but only with rigorous treatment.
   c. Almost half become antisocial adults.
   d. Most continue to demonstrate behavioral problems at least into early adulthood.

5. The strongest predictor of conduct disorder in sociological studies is
   a. mild mental retardation.
   b. poor neighborhood.
   c. large family.
   d. race.

6. Recent concerns over the safety of antidepressant medication in children have focused on
   a. tardive dyskinesia.
   b. suicidality.
   c. catatonic immobility.
   d. increased aggression.

7. Which of the following is not a learning disorder listed in the DSM-IV-TR?
   a. reading disorder
   b. disorder of oral expression
   c. disorder of written expression
   d. mathematics disorder

8. Recent findings on brain functioning among people with and without dyslexia have found
    a. differences in frontal lobe functioning.
    b. similarities in frontal lobe glucose metabolism.
    c. differences in certain cortical language areas during phonological processing tasks.
    d. all of the above are correct.

* 9. The identification of mental retardation is typically made
    a. before birth, through amniocentesis.
    b. during infancy.
    c. when the child starts school.
    d. when the child begins puberty.

* 10. What is a problem with current estimates regarding the long-term prognosis for autistic children?
    a. Studies of autistic adults rely on retrospective accounts.
    b. In the early studies, most autistic children died before reaching adulthood.
    c. Most autistic children and their families refuse to participate in research projects, resulting in biased, nonrepresentative samples.
    d. Long-term follow-up studies have not been done since the time when new laws have required educational programs for all autistic children.

Short Answer

1. Distinguish between ADHD and "rambunctious kid".

2. How effective are drug treatments for hyperactivity?

3. Describe what is done in family intervention with conduct-disordered children.

4. Four-year-old Jerry is very afraid of the dark. Explain why we should and should not be concerned.

5. Describe the approach to measuring mental retardation, that is encouraged by the American Association of Mental retardation.

6. Describe PKU as a cause of mental retardation.

7. Describe what is done in cognitive interventions for treating mental retardation.

8.   What is the fundamental symptom of autism?   Give several examples of this symptom.

9.   Describe results of research suggesting a genetic basis for autism.

10.   Describe the general approach to psychological treatment of autism.

Internet Resources

The following are Internet resources to begin exploring the topics in this chapter. Additional general Internet resources are at the end of the introduction chapter.

Autism Society of America (ASA) offers education and advocacy for families of individuals with autism spectrum disorders.   www.autism-society.org

American Association on Mental Retardation advocates and promotes the needs of people with mental retardation. The association's "fact sheets" are especially useful.   www.aamr.org

Children and adults with AD/HD is a non-profit organization providing information about AD/HD to parents, educators, professionals, the media, and the general public.   www.chadd.org

Clinical Practice Guideline: Diagnosis and Evaluation of the Child With Attention-Deficit/Hyperactivity Disorder illustrates the complexities of diagnosing ADHD.
aappolicy.aappublications.org/cgi/content/full/pediatrics%3b105/5/1158

Downs Syndrome website is compiled by both professionals and parents with information, resources, and links.   www.nas.com/downsyn

Federation of Families for Children's Mental Health (FFCMH) has links to local affiliates across the country.   www.ffcmh.org

Answers to Self-Test, Chapter 14

Multiple Choice

1. b (p. 450)   2. c (p. 456)   3. a (p. 458)   4. d (p. 462)
5. b (p. 465)   6. b (p. 470)   7. b (p. 474)   8. c (p. 475-476)
9. c (p. 479)   10. d (p. 489)

Short Answer

1.   Many children are active and rambunctious. ADHD is for extreme and persistent problems, not just kids who are more active than parents or teachers prefer. (p. 451)

2.   Drugs improve concentration and reduce behavioral problems, but have little effect on long-term academic achievement and have side-effects. (p. 457-458)

3.   Parental behavior management training emphasizing positive reinforcement of prosocial behavior plus time-outs, etc. for misbehavior. (p. 465-466)

4.   Jerry will probably outgrow his fear of the dark; however, he still suffers and he may not learn developmental skills because of his fear. (p. 471)

5.   Measure strengths and weaknesses in terms of support or remediation needed to achieve higher functioning. (p. 479-480)

6.   PKU is a genetic inability to process phenylalanine, an amino acid. Without special diet, phenylalanine accumulates in the body, producing brain damage and profound retardation. (p. 481-482)

7.   Children are taught to verbalize and carry out cognitive steps to solve problems. Teacher verbalizes cognitions while solving, then verbalizes while child solves, then child verbalizes while solves, etc. (p. 483-484)

8.   The fundamental symptom is extreme aloneness. For example, autistic children don't seem interested in or responsive to others; they don't look at people or respond to affection. (p. 485)

9.   Risk of autism rises dramatically in siblings of children with autism; up to 91% in identical twins. Non-autistic twins have autistic-like problems. (Researchers cannot do family studies as autistics rarely marry.) (p. 489-491)

10.   General approach is to involve the parents. Focus on increasing motivation and responsiveness rather than specific behaviors. Thus, parents let the child choose materials, provide natural reinforcers, and encourage attempts to respond even if the attempts are not correct. (p. 492)

15 Late Life and Psychological Disorders

Overview

Chapter 15 is the concluding chapter on developmental problems. Chapter 14 discussed disorders of childhood and growing up. Chapter 15 is devoted to the problems of aging and growing old. Both young and old people in our society are vulnerable. Others do not always think about their special circumstances and needs or provide the care and attention they may need. This is even more true for older than for younger people — a disturbing thought for those who anticipate living long enough to grow old.

Chapter 15 completes the text's discussion of specific psychological disorders. The next (and final) two chapters of the text deal more intensively with issues in abnormal psychology. Chapter 16 evaluates various treatment methods and discusses issues in integrating them. Treatment has been discussed throughout the text but Chapter 16 provides a more complete discussion. Finally, Chapter 17 will cover legal and ethical issues. Legal issues include issues regarding the insanity defense and commitment of disturbed individuals. Ethical issues cover rights of therapy clients and research participants. Earlier chapters have mentioned these topics in various contexts. The last two chapters bring together and complete these discussions.

Chapter Summary

Aging: Issues and Methods Until recently, the psychological problems of older people were neglected by mental health professionals. As life expectancy continues to improve, it will become even more important to learn about the disorders suffered by some older people and the most effective means of treating them.

Several stereotypes about aging are false. Generally, people in late life report low levels of negative emotion, are not inappropriately concerned with their health, and are not lonely. Moreover, they typically report active sexual lives. On the other hand, poverty, stigma, and physical disease are common challenges for people as they age.

In research studies, differences between a younger and an older group could reflect either cohort effects or effects of chronological age. Longitudinal studies are more helpful for making this distinction than cross-sectional studies are.

Cognitive Disorders in Late Life Serious cognitive disorders affect a small minority of older people. Two principal disorders have been distinguished: dementia and delirium.

In dementia, the person's intellectual functioning declines and memory, abstract thinking, and judgment deteriorate. If the dementia is progressive, as most are, the individual comes to seem like another person altogether and is, in the end, oblivious to his or her surroundings. A variety of diseases can cause this deterioration. The most common is Alzheimer's disease, a progressive, irreversible illness in which cortical cells waste away. Genes probably play some role in the etiology of Alzheimer's disease. A history of head injury and depression are also risk factors.

Other forms of dementia include frontal-temporal dementia, frontal-subcortical dementia, and dementia with Lewy bodies.

Dementia usually responds only minimally to medication treatment, but the person and the family affected by the disease can be counseled on how to make the remaining time manageable and even rewarding. If adequate support is given to caregivers, many patients can be looked after at home.

In delirium, there is sudden clouding of consciousness and other problems in thinking, feeling, and behaving: fragmented and undirected thought, incoherent speech, inability to sustain attention, hallucinations, illusions, disorientation, lethargy or hyperactivity, and mood swings. The condition is reversible, provided that the underlying cause is adequately treated. Causes include overmedication, infection of brain tissue, high fevers, malnutrition, dehydration, endocrine disorders, head trauma, cerebrovascular problems, and surgery.

Psychological Disorders in Late Life Data indicate that persons over age sixty-five have the lowest overall rates of mental disorders of all age groups. When older people experience psychological disorders, the symptoms are often a recurrence of a disorder that first emerged earlier in life.

In older adults, depression tends to be accompanied by more cognitive impairment. When the onset of a first episode of depression occurs after age 65, cardiovascular disease is often a cause.

More of the suicide attempts of old people result in death than do those of younger people, and the group with the highest rate of suicide is elderly Caucasian men.

Anxiety disorders are more prevalent than depression among older adults.

Delusional (paranoid) disorder may also be seen in older patients. Sometimes, onset occurs in the context of brain disorders, sensory losses, or increasing social isolation.

Medication treatments for psychological disorders are similar in effectiveness during adulthood and late life, but must be used with caution because the elderly are more sensitive to side effects and toxicity.

Issues Specific to Treatment with Older Adults The treatments shown to help most psychological disorders in adulthood appear to be helpful for late life disorders. For example, cognitive, behavioral, and interpersonal psychotherapy are effective for depression, and cognitive behavioral treatment is effective for anxiety.

Psychological treatments may need to be tailored to the needs of older people. Clinicians should sometimes be active and directive, providing information and seeking out the agencies that give the social services needed by their clients.

Living Situations: Community Living, Nursing Homes, and Other Alternatives Most older persons reside in the community.

Nursing homes sometimes do little to encourage residents to maintain whatever capacities they have. Both physical and mental deterioration may occur. Serious neglect can be found in some nursing homes, and access to mental health care is limited. Several efforts have been made to correct these deficiencies.

An increasingly popular alternative is assisted-living facilities.

Learning Goals

1. Be able to describe common misconceptions about age-related changes, and to describe genuine age-related changes.

2. Be able to discuss issues involved in conducting research on aging.

3. Be able to explain the symptoms of dementia and delirium, and understand current approaches to etiology and treatment.

4. Be able to describe the prevalence, etiology, and treatment of psychological disorders in the elderly.

5. Be able to explain the issues involved with community living, assisted living, and nursing homes.

Key Terms

Social selectivity (p. 499)

Age effects (p. 500)

Cohort effects (p. 500)

Time-of-measurement effects (p. 501)

Selective mortality (p. 501)

Dementia (p. 502)

Alzheimer's disease (p. 503)

Disorientation (p. 504)

Plaques (p. 504)

Neurofibrillary tangles (p. 504)

Frontal-temporal dementia [FTD] (p. 505)

Dementia with Lewy bodies [DLB] (p. 506)

Delirium (p. 509-510)

Study Questions

Aging: Issues and Methods (p. 497-502)

1.   How are older adults treated in the United States? Identify five myths about older people. How does diversity change as people age?   Identify medical problems experienced in late life involving sleep and prescription medication. (p. 497-500)

2.   Identify three effects that influence research on aging. Describe two research methods and a problem with each. (p. 500-501)

Cognitive Disorders in Late Life (p. 502-512)

3.   Define and distinguish between two kinds of cognitive disorders that may affect older people (starting on p. 502 and 509). Describe at least four common symptoms of dementia. What are the physiological changes and genetic factors in Alzheimer's? Describe symptoms and causes of four other kinds of dementia. (p. 502-507)

4.   Describe the standard medical treatment and two other medical approaches for dementia. Describe the role of supportive psychotherapy and approaches to managing memory decline, disruptive behavior, and cognitive limitations. (p. 507-509)

5.   Describe at least four common symptoms of delirium and distinguish them from symptoms of dementia. What are common causes? Why is diagnosis difficult and important? Describe methods for treating and preventing delirium. (p. 509-512)

Psychological Disorders in Late Life (p. 513-520)

6.   How common are psychological disorders in late life? Describe three methodological and one psychological explanation for this.   Why are medical issues important in diagnosing psychological problems? (p. 513-514)

7.   The text describes depression, suicide, anxiety, and delusional (paranoid) disorders. For each problem describe (a) how it differs in older people, (b) possible causes, and (c) treatment. Describe issues regarding substance abuse and medication abuse. (p. 514-520)

Adjusting Treatment with Older Adults (p. 520-521)

8.   Identify four barriers to treatment of older adults and three ways clinicians need to adjust their approach. (p. 520-521)

Living Situations: Community Living, Nursing Homes, and Other Alternatives
(p. 522-526)

9. What percentage of older adults live in the community?   What kinds of services are (sometimes) provided, and why is collaboration important? (p. 522-523)

10. What are common effects of nursing home placement on family caregivers? Summarize a study suggesting subtle problems in nursing home care and a possible reason for the results. More generally, what problems exist in many nursing homes despite government efforts?   Why is mental health care needed? (p. 523-526)

11. Describe two kinds of alternative living settings for older adults. (p. 526)

Self-Test, Chapter 15
(* Items not covered in Study Questions.)

Multiple Choice

* 1.   Cohort effects are an example of which problem in research?
       a. third variable
       b. directionality
       c. reliability
       d. longitudinal

2.   Alzeheimer's disease is largely related to
       a. neurotransmitter dysfunction.
       b. neurofibrillary tangles.
       c. loss of renal function.
       d. frontal lobe disturbances.

3.   Which of the following conditions is associated with Frontal-Temporal dementias?
       a. Pick's disease
       b. Huntington's chorea
       c. Parkinson's disease
       d. Delirium

4.   Delirium can be distinguished from dementia in that delirium is associated with
       a. forgetfulness, memory loss.
       b. poor social judgment.
       c. slow insidious onset.
       d. erratic, changing behavior.

5.   Which of the following is a likely contributor to the prevalence of major depression in older adults?
       a. stressful life events
       b. delirium
       c. retirement
       d. social isolation

6.   One of the medical concerns about using benzodiazapenes to treat anxiety disorders in older adults is
       a. cognitive decline.
       b. increased morbidity.
       c. urinary incontinence.
       d. all of the above.

7.   A problem in using the DSM-IV-TR to identify substance use problems in older adults is
       a. most older adults do not abuse substances.
       b. heavy drinkers consume less as they age, so the criteria could lead to underidentification.
       c. the criteria are sufficiently stringent that social drinking in older adults appears similar to substance abuse.
       d. tolerance increases with age; thus, older adults can safely consume more substances.

8.   Which of the following is a barrier that may prevent older people from receiving mental health care?
      a. negative beliefs about mental illness
      b. older people are less likely to be assessed and referred for mental health care
      c. financial concerns
      d. all of the above

* 9. A problem with mental health services in nursing homes
      a. is that the treatment recommendations are often not implemented.
      b. is that the services are limited to the treatment of dementia.
      c. is that interventions, both behavioral and medical, are rarely effective in elderly populations.
      d. is that most elderly people have negative attitudes toward mental health treatment and therefore refuse treatment.

* 10. The theory of mental and physical deterioration in the elderly as described by Langer is most similar to
      a. cognitive dissonance theory.
      b. learned helplessness theory.
      c. labeling theory.
      d. diathesis-stress theory.

Short Answer

1.   Are older people more similar or more different from each other compared to younger people? Explain briefly.

2.   What are the general issues in prescription medications for older people?

3.   As a method of studying older adults, describe "longitudinal studies" and a problem with them.

4.   You are a psychotherapist assigned to work with an older person with early Alzheimer's. What would you emphasize in working with them?

5.   Describe the treatment of delirium.

6.   Identify four reasons for the decline in psychological problems in older adults.

7. Why are medical issues especially important in diagnosing psychological problems in older adults?

8. Briefly describe the major issue in providing services to older adults in the community.

9. Summarize a study suggesting that even good-quality nursing home care may be undesirable.

10. Describe "assisted living" facilities for older adults.

Internet Resources

The following are internet resources to begin exploring the topics in this chapter. Additional general internet resources are at the end of the introduction chapter.

Alzheimer's Association is a non-profit organization offering information, support, and advocacy for individuals with Alzheimer's and their families. Includes links to local chapters and support groups.

www.alz.org

Delirium describes symptoms and distinctions between dementia and other syndromes.

www.emedicine.com/med/topic3006.htm

Answers to Self-Test, Chapter 15

Multiple Choice

1. a (p. 500-501)	2. b (p. 504)	3. a (p. 505-506)	4. d (p. 510)
5. a (p. 515)	6. d (p. 518)	7. b (p. 519-520)	8. d (p. 520)
9. a (p. 525)	10. b (p. 525)		

Short Answer

1. Despite stereotypes, older people are more diverse than younger. People become less alike as they age. (p. 499)

2. Physicians tend to prescribe medications to relieve complaints so that older people end up taking many medications. They may be prescribed medications to relieve side-effects of other medications. The metabolism of older people is less efficient so side-effects and toxic overdoses can easily occur. (p. 500)

3. Longitudinal studies retest the same people repeatedly over a long time. While they have advantages, a problem is that people drop out of the study due to death, infirmity, etc. [selective mortality], thus biasing the results. (p. 501)

4. Provide information and support for client and family. Provide techniques to manage declining memory and disruptive behaviors without demeaning or emphasizing limitations. (p. 507)

5. Important to diagnose delirium and treat the underlying cause (medication overdose, infection, etc.) to minimize long-term decline. Anti-psychotic drugs may be needed to manage symptoms. With treatment, complete recovery is likely. (p. 511-512)

6. Methodological reasons include that a) older adults may be less likely to admit symptoms, b) they grew up in less turbulent times [i.e. a cohort effect], and c) people with serious problems may have died. It also is likely that older adults have learned better coping skills over their lives. (p. 513-514)

7. Because medical conditions are more common in older adults and can produce symptoms that mimic psychological conditions. (p. 514)

8. Major issue is coordinating services. Too often, service agencies are hard to locate, have confusing or contradictory policies, etc. so that older adults do not get what they need and deteriorate. (p. 522)

9. Old people were randomly assigned to three intensities of professional care. Results showed that more intense professional involvement actually increased death rates (because the professionals pushed nursing home placement where early death was more likely). (p. 524)

10. Resemble hotels with suites for residents and dining rooms, daily activities, beauty shops, staff support, nursing and medical assistance, etc. Note that "continuing care retirement communities" provide a wider range of options including independent living, assisted living, and nursing home care. (p. 526)

16 Psychological Treatment

Overview

The previous chapter completed the text's discussion of major forms of abnormal behavior. Chapter 16 begins the last section of the text, which covers issues in abnormal psychology. These issues underlie many topics covered earlier and round out discussion of the field.

Chapter 16 discusses issues in psychological treatment. Psychological treatments for various disorders were covered in the chapters on those disorders. Chapter 16 discusses treatment approaches more systematically as well as efforts to integrate them. Chapter 17 deals with legal and ethical issues. Legal issues include insanity, competency to stand trial, and involuntary commitment. Ethical issues concern the rights of research participants and therapy clients.

Chapter Summary

Challenges in Evaluating Treatment Outcomes Research on the effectiveness of various forms of psychological treatments has been conducted for many decades. Overall, this research suggests that about 75 percent of people gain some improvement from therapy. Therapy also seems to be more helpful than a placebo or the passage of time.

Efforts have been made to define standards for research on psychotherapy trials and to summarize the current state of knowledge on which psychological treatments work. These standards typically include the need to randomly assign participants to treatment or a control, to use a treatment manual, to define the treated sample carefully, and to use reliable and valid outcome measures. It is hoped that these efforts will help disseminate the best available therapeutic practices to clinicians and their clients, as well as provide insurance companies with the data to support the use of psychotherapy.

Controversy exists about the research standards: a large proportion of clients are excluded or will not take part in clinical trials, cultural diversity is lacking in most trials, many treatment approaches remain untested, and treatment manuals could constrain a talented therapist. A broader concern is that a huge gap exists between what happens in the research world and the real world. Efficacy research focuses on how well therapies work in carefully controlled experiments, whereas effectiveness research focuses on how well therapies work in the real world.

The Importance of Culture and Ethnicity in Psychological Treatment Clinicians offering treatment to minority individuals must be sensitive to the values and political events that shape the way people may approach relationships, therapy, and emotional expression. Little empirical research is available on how psychotherapies work for people from diverse backgrounds, but minority status is associated with less use of therapy. Researchers have developed modifications of some treatments to be more culturally sensitive.

Specific Treatment Approaches: Issues and Treatment Outcome Research Experiential psychotherapies, based on humanistic and existential psychology, emphasize freedom to choose, personal growth, and personal responsibility. Variants of these approaches include Rogers's client-centered therapy, existential therapy, Gestalt therapy, and Emotion-focused therapy.

Treatment outcome research supports the efficacy of psychodynamic, experiential, and cognitive behavioral approaches compared to no treatment or treatment controls. Behavioral approaches offer a clear advantage for the treatment of anxiety and may be slightly more helpful than experiential approaches in other disorders. Generally, the literature on how these different active forms of psychotherapy compare to each other is quite small.

Cognitive behavioral treatments have evolved over the past 10 years, and several manuals incorporate broader themes such as spirituality and meaning. Although there is less research available, the research findings regarding cognitive behavioral treatments are promising.

Marital or couples therapy helps distressed couples resolve the inevitable conflicts in any ongoing relationship of two adults living together. Behavioral therapies are clearly better than no treatment, but within a matter of a couple years, at least half of couples return to significant distress. Promising evidence exists for integrative behavioral marital therapy and insight-oriented marital therapy as compared to standard behavioral marital therapy.

Family therapy includes many different techniques. These therapies have been shown to be particularly successful in the treatment of externalizing disorders in children and adolescents, in helping people with substance abuse accept the need for treatment, and in reducing relapse in adults with schizophrenia and bipolar disorder.

Psychotherapy Integration   There are three different approaches to therapy integration: technical eclecticism, theoretical integration, and common factorism. Technical eclecticism refers to borrowing techniques from other approaches while maintaining a focused conceptual approach. Theoretical integration is exemplified by Wachtel's cyclical psychodynamics, or by the recent inclusion of a focus on acceptance within cognitive behavioral therapies. Common factors research identifies variables that predict outcomes across a broad range of therapies, such as the quality of the therapeutic alliance or therapist empathy.

Community Psychology   Community psychology aims primarily at the prevention of disorder on a large-scale. Political issues have shaped the popularity of this approach over time.

Learning Goals

1.   Be able to explain standards for studies on psychotherapy, and the gaps in the generalizability of treatment outcome research.

2.   Be able to discuss issues in adapting psychotherapies for people from diverse ethnic and cultural backgrounds.

3.   Be able to identify the specific types of psychological treatments that have empirical support, as well as issues that clinicians must consider in applying these treatments.

4.   Be able to describe different approaches to integrating psychotherapies and identifying common elements across treatments.

5.   Be able to discuss the goals of community psychology and political trends in that field.

Key Terms

Empirically supported treatments [ESTs] (p. 530)

Outcome research (p. 530)

Randomized controlled trials [RCTs] (p. 530)

Efficacy (p. 533)

Effectiveness (p. 533)

Stepped care (p. 534)

Cultural competence (p. 535)

Empathy (p. 540)

Client-centered therapy (p. 541)

Self-actualization (p. 541)

Unconditional positive regard (p. 541)

Existential therapy (p. 541)

Gestalt therapy (p. 542)

Behavioral activation therapy (p. 544)

Paradoxical intervention (p. 546)

Reactance (p. 546)

Self-efficacy (p. 546)

Rational Emotive Behavior Therapy [REBT] (p. 547)

Technical eclecticism (p. 555)

Theoretical integration (p. 555)

Common factors (p. 556)

Process research (p. 557)

Therapeutic [working] alliance (p. 557)

Self-efficacy (p. 558)

Study Questions

Challenges in Evaluating Treatment Outcomes (p. 529-534)

1. Describe evidence on the effectiveness of psychotherapy. How are empirically supported treatments identified and shown to be specific? Describe their advantages and disadvantages in three areas. (p. 529-534)

The Importance of Culture and Ethnicity in Psychological Treatment (p. 535-538)

2.   Discuss two general issues in how well therapy works with people from different ethnic backgrounds. For three ethnic groups, identify two or three issues for therapists. Describe how researchers are studying therapy with specific ethnic groups and ways they are adapting treatment approaches. (p. 535-538)

Specific Treatment Approaches: Issues and Outcome Research (p. 539-554)

3.   Explain two basic issues in evaluating the effectiveness of psychoanalysis. For traditional psychoanalytic treatment, identify three general conclusions, one problem, and results of an ambitious study. For brief psychoanalytic treatments, identify one general conclusion, comparison to other treatments, and one controversy. (p. 539-540)

4.   The text describes four experiential therapies. What is the core emphasis of all four? For client-centered therapy, identify six assumptions and two techniques. For Existential therapy, describe views on anxiety, responsibility, and aloneness. For Gestalt therapy, describe views on accepting inner desire insights and the "here and now". For Emotion-focused therapy, describe two kinds of emotions and the goal of therapy. How effective are these approaches, and why is it hard to compare them to cognitive behavioral therapies? (p. 540-544)

5.   Describe the method and effectiveness of four behavioral therapies (exposure, rewards and punishments, behavioral activation, and childhood problems). Explain why maintaining gains is important and two ways of achieving this goal. (p. 544-545)

6.   Explain the basic assumption of all cognitive behavioral therapies. Identify differences between Beck and Ellis in terms of their views and styles. Describe Marlatt's relapse prevention therapy. Describe two new themes in the third wave of cognitive behavioral therapy. Summarize outcome research including overall effectiveness, range of problems, effects of intelligence, and continued improvement. (p. 545-550)

7.   Describe couples therapy by describing two common couple problems and three common techniques. Identify five conclusions of couples therapy outcome research. How has adding emotional and insight components affected outcomes in behavioral couples therapy? (p. 550-551)

8. What is the general assumption of family therapy, and how is it adapted for different problems? Describe its effectiveness. (p. 553-554)

Psychotherapy Integration (p. 554-558)

9. What is the rationale for and against eclecticism? Describe two approaches to eclecticism and an argument against the second approach.   Explain common factors and process research as a third approach to eclecticism.   As an example, describe research on the therapeutic alliance including results and three reasons for them.   Summarize process research on other treatment predictors illustrating why this research is so difficult to conduct. (p. 555-558)

Community Psychology and Prevention Science (p. 559-561)

10. What is the basic goal of community psychology? Identify two reasons community psychology is difficult to evaluate. Summarize two political factors that contributed to the growth of community psychology and two that contributed to its decline. (p. 559-561)

Self-Test, Chapter 16

(* Items not covered in Study Questions.)

Multiple Choice

1. Most researchers involved in outcome research agree that a treatment study should include the following:
    a. random assignment of subjects to treatment comparison conditions.
    b. reliable and valid outcome data.
    c. inclusion of a control or comparison treatment condition.
    d. all of the above.

2. Treatment manuals allow for
    a. greater external validity.
    b. less external validity.
    c. less reliability.
    d. greater internal validity.

* 3. Jason begins to see a clinical psychologist in order to treat his anxiety in social situations. His psychologist begins by treating Jason's problem with the least expensive treatment. This treatment strategy is called
    a. humanistic therapy.
    b. stepped care.
    c. systematic desensitization.
    d. multisystemic treatment.

4. Hector is Latino and holds traditional values. He seeks therapy for depression associated with job stress. Which type of therapy will likely benefit him most?
    a. cognitive behavioral therapy
    b. traditional psychodynamic therapy
    c. gestalt therapy
    d. Any of these would be fine as long as the therapist is culturally competent.

5. The aim of existential therapy is to
    a. self-actualize.
    b. confront one's anxieties concerning life choices.
    c. be able to express oneself accurately.
    d. develop unconditional positive regard for oneself.

6. A particular problem with behavioral therapies is
    a. convincing the client to "buy into" the idea of contingencies.
    b. maintaining gains after therapy ends.
    c. finding therapists who are willing to conduct them.
    d. they are not effective with children.

7.   Which of the following statements is <u>false</u>?
     a. Couples therapists often use videotape equipment to help couples better understand their communication patterns.
     b. Couples therapists often give homework assignments in which the couples are asked to practice new interaction patterns.
     c. Couples therapists are behavioral and tend to conceptualize interactions patterns in this light.
     d. Couples therapists choose specific techniques to match their theoretical orientation.

8.   Family therapy has been found to be effective in reducing the symptoms of
     a. borderline personality disorder.
     b. bipolar disorder.
     c. gender identity disorder.
     d. all of the above.

9.   Wachtel argues that behavior therapists should
     a. seek to modify behavior in order to uncover unconscious processes.
     b. be attuned to unconscious motivations.
     c. examine the meaning behind their interventions.
     d. all of the above.

10. Community psychology aims to
     a. reduce environmental risks for a disorder.
     b. bolster protective factors against a disorder.
     c. both a and b are correct.
     d. neither a nor b are correct.

Short Answer

1.   Explain two basic issues in evaluating classical psychoanalysis.

2.   According to research, how effective are brief psychoanalytic treatments?

3.   What are characteristics of healthy people according to Carl Rogers' client-centered therapy?

4.   Describe behavioral activation therapy.

5.   Distinguish between the therapeutic styles of Beck and Ellis.

6.   What is "mindfulness" as a theme in the third wave of cognitive behavioral therapy?

7.   Summarize the effectiveness of behavioral couples therapy and the effects of adding emotion and insight components.

8.   Summarize the general assumption of family therapy.

9.   Why is process research on treatment predictors so difficult?

10.   Identify two reasons that community psychology is hard to evaluate.

Internet Resources

The following are internet resources to begin exploring the topics in this chapter. Additional general internet resources are at the end of the introduction chapter.

About Psychotherapy offers practical information on forms of psychotherapy and therapists, when to consider therapy, when to stop, and other consumer information.   www.aboutpsychotherapy.com

APA Help Center has consumer information on psychological issues and treatment from the American Psychological Association.   helping.apa.org

DrugDigest has information on a wide range of drugs and supplements including side-effects and interactions.   www.drugdigest.org

Answers to Self-Test, Chapter 16

Multiple Choice

1. d (p. 530)	2. d (p. 532)	3. b (p. 534)	4. a (p. 536)
5. b (p. 541)	6. b (p. 544)	7. c (p. 550)	8. b (p. 554)
9. d (p. 555-556)	10. c (p. 559)		

Short Answer

1. One issue is how to measure outcome. Psychoanalysts prefer methods (like projective tests) that conventional researchers reject. Second issue is how to define a treatment and distinguish it from other psychoanalytic methods. (p. 539)

2. Generally, they are moderately effective, although the research is inconsistent. (p. 540)

3. Rogers says healthy people are aware of the reasons for their behavior; they are innately good and effective. They are purposive and goal directed. (p. 541)

4. It is a behavioral technique in which depressed people are urged to become more active and involved in activities that provide opportunities for positive reinforcement. (p. 544)

5. Beck is more supportive and interactive. He discusses with clients and builds rapport. Ellis is more forceful, didactic and confrontive. He lectures clients and forcefully points out irrationality. (P.S. It may help to know that Beck is from Philadelphia and Ellis is from New York City.) (p. 547)

6. Client is taught to be "mindful" regarding feelings; that is, to be very aware of emotions without responding immediately and impulsively to them. (p. 548-549)

7. Behavioral couples therapy has been effective, but not as effective as one might hope. Adding emotion and insight components appears to improve effectiveness. (p. 551)

8. Assumption is that family members influence each other. Thus, family patterns affect a family member's problem and, in turn, a problem in a family member affects the entire family. (p. 553)

9. It is difficult to identify the key process. Changing one thing (cognitions, behaviors, etc.) may change other things. A therapeutic technique may work by having an effect on some process beside the one targeted. (p. 558)

10. Community psychology seeks to prevent problems in the community. It is difficult to apply research controls to a community. Also, it's difficult to follow large numbers of people, and many participants drop out. (p. 559-560)

17 Legal and Ethical Issues

Overview

The last section of the text consists of two chapters discussing issues in abnormal psychology. The previous chapter, Chapter 16, covered issues in psychological treatment. It reviewed approaches to treatment and attempts to integrate them. This chapter, the final chapter of the text, turns to legal and ethical issues in abnormal psychology. While studying this chapter, remember that "issues" do not have easy solutions: if they did, they wouldn't be "issues". Especially when working with human beings, there are often no easy answers. Thus, it is important for psychologists to anticipate issues and to understand the various aspects, implications, and options involved in order to handle them as effectively as possible.

Chapter Summary

Some civil liberties are rather routinely set aside when mental health professionals and the courts judge that mental illness has played a decisive role in determining an individual's behavior. This may occur through criminal or civil commitment.

Criminal Commitment Criminal commitment sends a person to a hospital either before a trial for an alleged crime, because the person is deemed incompetent to stand trial, or after an acquittal by reason of insanity.

Several landmark cases and principles in law address the conditions under which a person who has committed a crime might be excused from legal responsibility for it—that is, not guilty by reason of insanity. These involve the presence of an irresistible impulse, the notion that some people may not be able to distinguish between right and wrong (the M'Naghten rule), and the principle that a person should not be held criminally responsible if his or her unlawful act is the product of mental disease or mental defect (the Durham principle). The Insanity Defense Reform Act of 1984 made it harder for accused criminals to argue insanity as an excusing condition.

Today, guilty but mentally ill, is in use in a number of states. This emergent legal doctrine reflects an uneasiness in legal and mental health circles about not holding people ascriptively responsible for crimes for which they are descriptively responsible.

There is an important difference between mental illness and insanity. The latter is a legal concept. A person can be diagnosed as mentally ill and yet be deemed sane enough both to stand trial and to be found guilty of a crime.

Civil Commitment A person who is considered mentally ill and dangerous to self and to others, although he or she has not broken a law, can be civilly committed to an institution or be allowed to live outside of a hospital, but only under supervision and with restrictions placed on his or her activities.

Recent court rulings have provided greater protection to all committed mental patients, particularly those under civil commitment. They have the right to written notification, to counsel, to a jury decision concerning their commitment, and to Fifth Amendment protection against self-incrimination;

the right to the least restrictive treatment setting; the right to be treated; and in most circumstances, the right to refuse treatment, particularly any procedure that entails considerable risk. However, there is a trend toward preventive detention when, for example, convicted sexual predators are about to be released from prison with every indication that they will harm others again.

Ethical Issues in Therapy and Research Ethical issues concerning research include restraints on what kinds of research are allowable and the duty of scientists to obtain informed consent from prospective human participants.

In the area of therapy, ethical issues concern the right of clients to confidentiality, the question of who is the client (for example, an individual or the state mental hospital that is paying the clinician) and the question of who sets the therapy goals.

Diagnosis of sexual abuse in childhood based on so-called recovered memories has also presented ethical problems, as well as legal dilemmas, for therapists.

Learning Goals

1.   Be able to differentiate the legal concepts of insanity and the various standards for the insanity defense.

2.   Be able to describe the issues surrounding competency to stand trial.

3.   Be able to delineate the conditions under which a person can be committed to a hospital under civil law.

4.   Be able to discuss the difficulties associated with predicting dangerousness and the issues surrounding the rights to receive and refuse treatment.

5.   Be able to describe the ethics surrounding psychological research and therapy.

Key Terms

Criminal commitment (p. 564)

Civil commitment (p. 564)

Insanity defense (p. 565)

Not guilty by reason of insanity [NGRI] (p. 565)

Guilty but mentally ill [GBMI] (p. 566)

Irresistible impulse (p. 566)

M'Naghten rule (p. 566)

Durham test (p. 567)

American Law Institute guidelines (p. 567-568)

Descriptive responsibility (p. 569)

Ascriptive responsibility (p. 569)

Competency to stand trial (p. 573)

In absentia (p. 574)

Outpatient commitment (p. 582)

Least restrictive alternative (p. 586)

Advanced directive (p. 591)

Informed consent (p. 596)

Confidentiality (p. 597)

Privileged communication (p. 597)

Study Questions

Criminal Commitment (p. 564-579)

1. What legal assumption underlies the concept of insanity? Describe two current types of laws regarding insanity in terms of legal findings and consequences. Trace the history of the insanity defense using four landmark cases and guidelines. (p. 564-568)

2. Describe the reason for and changes made by the Insanity Defense Reform Act and guilty but mentally ill laws. Summarize the case of *Jones v. United States* and the Supreme Court's decision. List four problems with insanity illustrated by this case. (p. 568-573)

3. Distinguish between "insanity" and "competency". What is the legal rationale behind competency and the legal grounds on which competency is evaluated? What are the consequences of being found incompetent and the issues underlying "synthetic sanity"? Explain two issues underlying insanity, mental retardation, and capital punishment and illustrate their implications. (p. 573-579)

Civil Commitment (p. 580-592)

4.   For civil commitment, describe the underlying principle, common criteria, and common categories of commitment procedures. (p. 580)

5.   How dangerous are former mental patients?   Describe and evaluate traditional research on predicting dangerousness.   Describe current criteria and practices to reduce potential violence. How have these principles been extended in the case of sex offenders? (p. 581-583)

6.   Summarize recent trends in voluntary/involuntary hospital admissions. How are courts protecting rights of individuals threatened with commitment? (p. 583-586)

7.   Summarize three recent trends in protecting the rights of individuals who have been committed including the case of *O'Connor v. Donaldson*. How do free will issues underlie these trends? Identify one way to reconcile these rights. What was the rationale behind deinstitutionalization, and what has been the result? (p. 586-592)

Ethical Dilemmas in Therapy and Research (p. 593-601)

8.   Distinguish between the approaches of science and of ethics and two ways in which the behaviors of scientists are regulated. Give three examples outside psychology that point to the need for ethical restraints in research. In current psychological research, what process protects participants? In current biomedical research, describe two issues. (p. 593-596)

9.   Within psychology, summarize five ethical dilemmas (starting with "Informed Consent"). Explain why each is a dilemma (i.e. why the ethically correct choice may be hard to identify) (p. 596-599). Distinguish, especially, between confidentiality and privileged communication (on p. 597)

10.   Summarize the textbook's concluding comments. (p. 600)

Self-Test, Chapter 17

(* Items not covered in Study Questions.)

Multiple Choice

1. Which of the following statements is true?
    a. If a person is mentally ill, they are rarely held responsible for a crime.
    b. A person can be diagnosed as mentally ill and still be held responsible for a crime.
    c. One of the main disputes in the Not Guilty by Reason of Insanity plea is figuring out whether or not the person actually committed the crime.
    d. All fifty states allow the insanity defense.

2. Which of the following is <u>not</u> a standard for determining insanity?
    a. did not understand the law
    b. irresistible impulse
    c. did not know right from wrong
    d. product of mental disease or defect

3. The trial of John Hinckley Jr. led to
    a. recognition of the need to protect the rights of mentally ill prisoners.
    b. concern about the illogic of finding someone who was sane at the time of a crime to be "not competent to stand trial."
    c. public outcry against the insanity defense.
    d. a push to begin applying the "not guilty by reason of insanity" rule.

* 4. Thomas Szasz asserts that the insanity defense should be
    a. made more clear.
    b. broadened.
    c. narrowed.
    d. eliminated.

* 5. Which of the following legal outcomes is <u>most</u> common?
    a. A person successfully uses the insanity defense to avoid imprisonment.
    b. A person is released from a psychiatric hospital sooner than he would have been released from prison because he or she used the insanity defense.
    c. A person is confined to a prison hospital because he or she is judged incompetent to stand trial.
    d. None of the above are common.

6. David has been found guilty of a murder and has been diagnosed with schizophrenia. Which of the following would mostly likely prevent David from receiving the death penalty?
    a. David is voluntarily taking medication.
    b. David's symptoms of schizophrenia have been unresponsive to medication.
    c. David agrees to enter psychotherapy in a facility of the criminally insane.
    d. David is mentally retarded.

7. Monahan suggests that the prediction of violence is most accurate under which of the following conditions?
    a. in non-emergency situations
    b. when the person is currently in the hospital because of past dangerous behavior
    c. in an emergency situation, when the person appears prepared to commit violence
    d. when a person can be evaluated over a period of time by a number of professionals in a controlled environment

8. "Right to refuse treatment" involves the rights of
    a. patients to refuse hospitalization.
    b. patients to refuse dangerous drugs.
    c. hospitals to refuse to treat dangerous patients.
    d. hospitals to refuse optimal treatment as long as they provide basic care.

9. The deinstitutionalization of mental patients was brought about because
    a. innovative community programs were being developed in large numbers.
    b. institutions were increasingly viewed as being warehouses, inadequate for truly treating the mentally ill.
    c. of the high cost of maintaining patients in institutions.
    d. of the impact of riots by involuntarily committed psychiatric patients.

10. Confidentiality and privileged communication can be distinguished in that only privileged communication legally protects individuals from
    a. being judged dangerous based on what they said.
    b. unethical practices of the therapist.
    c. having what they said revealed in court.
    d. being sued by the therapist for their statements.

Short Answer

1. Summarize the case of *Jones v. United States*.

2. What issues underlie synthetic sanity?

3. What is the underlying legal principle of civil commitment?

4. Suppose a friend of yours is considering suicide, but refuses to seek help. What should you do?

5. How dangerous are former mental patients?

6.   Describe two ways in which the behavior of scientists is regulated.

7.   In current psychological research what procedure protects the rights of research participants?

8.   Give four reasons why therapists may reveal things clients tell them even though state law provides privileged communication for therapy relationships.

9.   Describe the ethical issue of "who is the client".

10.   What is the ethical issue in reports of recovered memories of child abuse?

Internet Resources

The following are internet resources to begin exploring the topics in this chapter. Additional general internet resources are at the end of the introduction chapter.

American Association of Psychiatry and the Law has information on careers and issues on legal/mental health (forensic) areas.   www.aapl.org

Bazelon Center for Mental Health Law is a national legal advocate for people with mental disabilities.   www.bazelon.org

Answers to Self-Test, Chapter 17

Multiple Choice

1. b (p. 566)	2. a (p. 566-567)	3. c (p. 568)	4. d (p. 570)
5. c (p. 574)	6. d (p. 577-578)	7. c (p. 582)	8. b (p. 589)
9. b (p. 591-592)	10. c (p. 597)		

Short Answer

1. Jones was arrested for a misdemeanor but was found insane. As a result, he was hospitalized for longer than he would have been imprisoned if he had been found guilty. Supreme Court ruled it did not matter, as he was being treated, not punished. (p. 571-572)

2. Drugs could be used to make a person synthetically sane to stand trial. However the drugs might not work, might produce dangerous side effects, might give the jury a false impression, etc. (p. 575)

3. The underlying principle is the duty of government to protect citizens from harm, including harm they might do to themselves as well as harm to others. (p. 580)

4. Call the police who will pick up your friend and take him/her to a mental hospital to be evaluated for informal civil commitment. (Hopefully your friend will understand why you did this once he/she recovers; if not, at least he or she is still alive.) (p. 580)

5. Despite stereotypes, research indicates they are, generally, no more dangerous than other people. The exception is substance abusers, who are more likely to be dangerous (whether ex-patients or not). (p. 581)

6. The two ways are laws and ethical codes of professional groups. (p. 594-595)

7. Research proposals are reviewed for safety and ethical propriety by institutional review boards in the hospital, school, etc. The boards include non-psychologist members. (p. 595)

8. (a) Client accuses the therapist of malpractice, (b) client is being abused, (c) client started therapy to evade law, and (d) client is dangerous to self or others. (p. 597)

9. The term refers to situations in which the therapist has responsibility to several individuals or entities whose interests may differ, such as a client and a company. The therapist may not be able to serve both interests. (p. 597-598)

10. There are dangers both in encouraging and discouraging clients to recover memories. Encouragement could lead to false diagnosis. Discouragement could mean the memory remains repressed but hampers the client's current life. (p. 598-599)